Tomorrow's Geog
for Edexcel GCSE Specification A
REVISION GUIDE

Unit 2 The Natural Environment

Mike Harcourt
Steph Warren

DYNAMIC
LEARNING

HODDER
EDUCATION
AN HACHETTE UK COMPANY

Every effort has been made to trace all copyright holders, but if any have been inadvertently overlooked the Publishers will be pleased to make the necessary arrangements at the first opportunity.

The publishers would like to thank the following for permission to reproduce copyright material:

page 7 © David McNew/Getty Images News, **page 11** Mike Harcourt, **page 18** Steph Warren, **page 28** © Fabrice Coffrini/AFP/Getty Images, **page 29** Mike Harcourt, **page 39** © Copyright 2006 SASI Group (University of Sheffield) and Mark Newman (University of Michigan) (www.worldmapper.org), **page 40** *tl, tr, br* Wikimedia Commons, **page 42** © www.CartoonStock.com, **page 49** © GRID-Arendal. Philippe Rekacewicz (Le Monde diplomatique) http://maps.grida.no/go/graphic/freshwater-use-by-sector-at-the-beginning-of-the-2000s/ (source: based on data from Table FW1 in *World Resources 2000–2001, People and Ecosystems: The Fraying Web of Life*, World Resources Institute (WRI), Washington DC, 2000).

Although every effort has been made to ensure that website addresses are correct at time of going to press, Hodder Education cannot be held responsible for the content of any website mentioned in this book. It is sometimes possible to find a relocated web page by typing in the address of the home page for a website in the URL window of your browser.

Hachette UK's policy is to use papers that are natural, renewable and recyclable products and made from wood grown in sustainable forests. The logging and manufacturing processes are expected to conform to the environmental regulations of the country of origin.

Orders: please contact Bookpoint Ltd, 130 Milton Park, Abingdon, Oxon OX14 4SB. Telephone: (44) 01235 827720. Fax: (44) 01235 400454. Lines are open 9.00–5.00, Monday to Saturday, with a 24-hour message-answering service. Visit our website at www.hoddereducation.co.uk.

© Mike Harcourt and Steph Warren 2010

First published in 2003 by Hodder Education,
An Hachette UK Company
338 Euston Road,
London NW1 3BH

This second edition published 2010

Impression number   5
Year   2014 2013 2012

Illustrations by Pantek Arts, Countryside Illustrations and Gray Publishing
Produced and typeset in 11/13pt Myriad by Gray Publishing, Tunbridge Wells
Printed in India

A catalogue record for this title is available from the British Library

ISBN: 978 0340 98797 1

Contents

Unit 2 The Natural Environment

1   Coastal Landscapes

Coastal processes produce landforms

What types of waves are there?

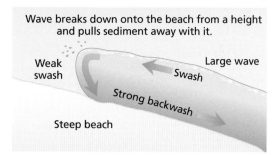

Wave breaks down onto the beach from a height and pulls sediment away with it.

Weak swash
Large wave
Swash
Strong backwash
Steep beach

Figure 1a A destructive wave

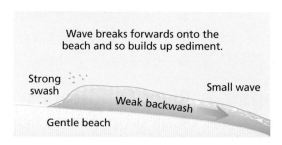

Wave breaks forwards onto the beach and so builds up sediment.

Strong swash
Small wave
Weak backwash
Gentle beach

Figure 1b A constructive wave

What are the main types of weathering?

Weathering: ways that rocks are broken down

Physical weathering: freeze–thaw action

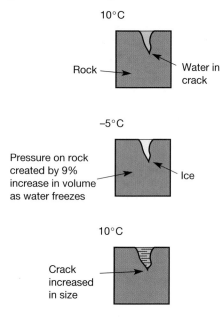

10°C
Rock
Water in crack

−5°C
Pressure on rock created by 9% increase in volume as water freezes
Ice

10°C
Crack increased in size

Figure 2 Main types of weathering

Biological weathering

Seed falls into crack
↓
Rain causes seedling to grow
↓
Roots force their way into cracks
↓
As the roots grow they break up the rock

Burrowing animals also break up rock.

Chemical weathering

Rainwater contains natural acids.

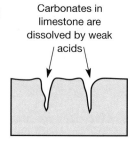

Carbonates in limestone are dissolved by weak acids

Cracks in rock expand

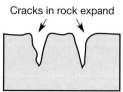

How are coasts eroded?

Corrasion – sand and pebbles carried in waves are thrown against the cliff face.
Corrosion – chemicals in sea water dissolve certain rock types, such as chalk.
Hydraulic action – the compression of air in cracks which puts pressure on the rock and causes pieces of the rock to break off.

The following are processes that are happening in the sea:
Attrition – the breaking up of rocks and pebbles in the waves.
Transportation – the movement of sand and pebbles by the sea.
Deposition – the putting down of sand and pebbles by the sea.

What is mass movement?

Mass movement: when material moves down a slope, pulled by gravity

Soil creep
- Slowest downhill movement.
- Gravity pulls water in the soil downhill.
- Soil particles move with the water.
- Heavy rainfall causes faster downhill movement.
- The slope appears to have ripples.
- The ripples are known as terracettes.

Slumping
- A large area of land moving down a slope.
- Common on clay cliffs.
- Dry weather makes the clay contract and crack.
- When it rains, water gets into the cracks.
- The soil becomes saturated.
- A large piece of rock is pulled down the cliff face.
- It has slipped on the slip plane of saturated rock.

What landforms are created by coastal erosion?

Erosional features – cliffs and wave-cut platforms

In these boxes the explanation is underlined.

Above the wave-cut notch an overhang develops. As the notch becomes larger the overhang will become unstable. This is because of its weight and the lack of support. In time the overhang will fall due to the pull of gravity.

As the width of the platform increases the power of the sea decreases, because it has further to travel to reach the cliff and the water is shallower causing more friction.

In this box the process explanation is in bold.

The cliff is eroded at the bottom by **corrasion. This is pebbles carried by the sea which are thrown against the cliff by the breaking wave, knocking off parts of the cliff.** In time a wave-cut notch is formed.

The sea continues to attack the cliff in this way and the cliff retreats.

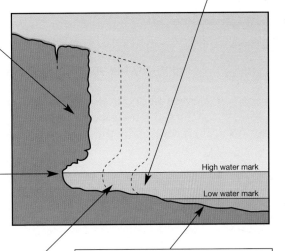

High water mark

Low water mark

The remains of the cliff, now below the sea at high tide, form a rocky wave-cut platform. The platform will also contain the boulders which have fallen from the cliff.

Erosional features – headlands and bays

These form due to different rock types.

- Only occur on coastlines where soft and hard rocks are found at right angles to the sea.
- The soft rock erodes more quickly than the hard rock forming bays.
- The hard rock is more resistant and sticks out as headlands.
- There should also be reference to the processes of erosion.

A* grade candidates may also refer to the fact that erosion eventually becomes greater on the headlands because the bays have retreated and the headlands are more exposed. The sea is not as powerful in the bays because it is shallower and therefore starts to deposit material.

ACTIVITY

Explain the formation of headlands and bays. After you have completed your answer, underline the process explanation in one colour and the sequence explanation in another.

The formation of caves, arches, stacks and stumps

This is just description.

A stump is formed by the action of the sea and weathering. The sea erodes a crack using hydraulic action and makes it bigger, forming a cave. If it is a headland, caves will form on either side. Eventually the backs of the caves meet and an arch is formed. In time the arch will collapse forming a stack. The stack will then collapse forming a stump.

Below is an A* answer that explains how a stump is formed. Note the comments, which pick out the sequence description, explanation and the processes.

Sequence description → A stump is formed by the action of the sea and weathering.

Process explanation → The sea erodes a crack with hydraulic action. This is when water hits the cliff compressing air in cracks. As the water retreats the pressure is released breaking off pieces of rock.

Sequence description → This makes the crack bigger forming a cave. If it is a headland, caves will form on either side. Eventually the backs of the caves meet and an arch is formed. In time the arch will collapse forming a stack.

Process explanation → This is due to undercutting of the sea. One of the processes the sea uses is corrasion which is when rocks in the sea are thrown against the cliff breaking off pieces of the cliff.

Sequence explanation → The arch becomes wider at the bottom and is unable to support the weight above. Eventually the arch is pulled down by gravity.

Sequence and process → Weathering is also active on the cliff face and further weakens the cliff. Through time the sea erodes the bottom of the stack and it collapses to leave a stump, which is covered by the sea at high tide.

This is a C grade answer. Again the sequence description, explanation and processes are picked out.

Process
Sequence described
Sequence explained
→ A stack is formed by the action of the sea. The sea erodes a crack in the cliff using corrasion. Eventually the cave becomes an arch. In time the arch will collapse forming a stack. This is due to undercutting of the sea. The arch becomes wider at the bottom and is unable to support the weight above. Eventually the arch is pulled down by gravity.

Read the question carefully. Have you been asked to describe or explain?

You must include sequence and processes on all landform formation questions.

Don't forget, a diagram will always help your answer.

What landforms are created by coastal deposition?

Depositional features – beaches

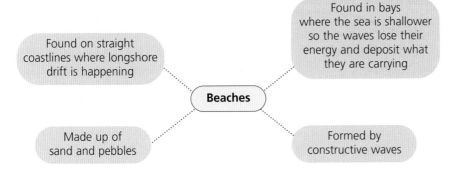

Found on straight coastlines where longshore drift is happening

Found in bays where the sea is shallower so the waves lose their energy and deposit what they are carrying

Beaches

Made up of sand and pebbles

Formed by constructive waves

Depositional features – spits and bars

- Spits are narrow stretches of sand and pebbles that are joined to the land at one end.
- If you are asked to explain the formation of a bar you need to discuss spit formation and then add the following points.
- Bars are spits which go across a bay.
- This is only possible if there is shallow water and no river entering the sea.

What is longshore drift?

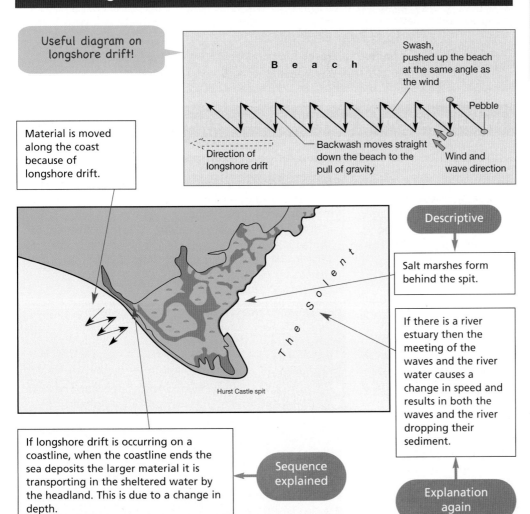

Useful diagram on longshore drift!

B e a c h

Swash, pushed up the beach at the same angle as the wind

Pebble

Direction of longshore drift

Backwash moves straight down the beach to the pull of gravity

Wind and wave direction

Material is moved along the coast because of longshore drift.

Descriptive

Salt marshes form behind the spit.

The Solent

If there is a river estuary then the meeting of the waves and the river water causes a change in speed and results in both the waves and the river dropping their sediment.

Hurst Castle spit

If longshore drift is occurring on a coastline, when the coastline ends the sea deposits the larger material it is transporting in the sheltered water by the headland. This is due to a change in depth.

Sequence explained

Explanation again

Coastal landforms are subject to change

Hint! You've already learnt these – look back to page 2 in this revision guide.

Why do some cliffs erode faster than others?

What affects the rate of coastal erosion?
The rate at which a cliff recedes depends on processes including erosion, weathering and mass movement. The rate at which these processes happen depends on fetch, geology and coastal management.

Fetch
The fetch is the distance that wind travels over open water.
● The longer the fetch the stronger the wave.

Geology
This is the rock type and structure of an area.
● Rock type – harder rocks, e.g. granite, are eroded more slowly. Think of headlands and bays!
● Rock angle to the coast – parallel or at right angles.

Coastal management
If a coastline is defended then it will erode much more slowly.
● Think of Walton.

Exam Tip

● Read the question carefully and don't get caught out.
● Remember to apply the correct mark scheme for your tier.

Foundation Tier
For questions that ask for examples, your answer will be marked as follows:
● Each point will receive a mark.
● If your answer does not contain specific points about an example you will lose one mark.

Higher Tier
For questions that ask for examples, your answer will be marked as follows:
● Each point will receive a mark.
● If your answer does not include specific points about an example you will only receive half marks.
● If examples are asked for and you only give one you will lose a mark.

ACTIVITY

Read the examples about coastal recession below. Try and answer the following question from memory:
Explain the effects of coastal recession. Use examples in your answer.

What are the effects of coastal recession on people and the environment?

The effects of coastal recession should be studied through a range of examples.

A doomed village! Happisburgh
Since 1995 25 properties and the village's lifeboat launching station have been lost to the sea. The village contains 18 listed buildings including a Grade 1 listed church which is estimated to be in the sea by 2020. The life of the villagers is totally dominated by their struggle against the sea.

Golfers paradise threatened!
A number of golf courses around the country are losing precious greens and fairways to the sea.
○ Sheringham in Norfolk is soon to lose its 5th and 6th holes
○ The Royal North Devon Golf Club at Westward Ho! is losing its 7th and 8th holes.

Tower's days are numbered!
The Tower at Walton-on-the-Naze could soon be lost to the sea if the cliff continues to erode at its present rate of 1.5 m a year. The area around the Tower is used for recreational purpose and is not deemed worthy of coastal protection.

Barton on Sea becomes Barton in the sea!
Since 1975 Barton has lost the following properties to the sea:
● Seaside café demolished because it had become dangerous.
● Manor Lodge demolished before it fell into the sea.
● 2004 coastal footpath closed; re-sited further back from cliff edge.
The area has had defences put in place as an effect of the erosion. The foot of the cliff below the Cliff House Hotel has been protected with rip-rap.
Most of the area within 100 m of the cliff has been left as recreational land or car parking to allow for future coastal recession.

Train passengers get a shower!
Passengers on the train travelling from Exeter to Plymouth and Penzance regularly get a shower as the sea washes over the tracks. On one occasion 160 passengers were stranded in a train for 4 hours while the sea washed over them because the train's electrics were not working.

How are the effects of coastal flooding reduced by prediction and prevention?

This should be studied through forecasting, building design, planning and education.

Forecasting
● The Met Office predicts (forecasts) the likelihood of a flood. The information gets to householders through weather forecasts and news broadcasts on the TV and radio. It is also on their website.
● The Environment Agency monitors sea conditions 24 hours a day, 365 days a year. This Storm Tide Forecasting Service provides forecasts of coastal flooding. Information is provided on a 24-hour Flood hotline and the Environment Agency's website.

Building design
● In Bangladesh all one-storey or two-storey buildings must have an external staircase to the roof.
● Houses along the coast at Malibu, near Los Angeles in California, are built on stilts to protect them from storm tides.
● Houses should minimise penetration from wind, rain and storms.

Education
Countries are now educating their citizens about what to do if a flood occurs.
● The government gives advice to the public via its website. There is general advice on how to protect their homes from flooding and what to do if a flood occurs.
● In Bangladesh many coastal areas have flood-warning systems.
● In King's Lynn in Norfolk there is a flood siren and people are employed by the council to go from house to house to warn people and help them to prepare.

Planning
Many countries have planned for coastal flooding by protecting themselves. For example:
● Before building takes place a full check must be made to ensure that the area is not prone to flooding. Planning permission will not be granted if it is.
● The Thames Flood Barrier was completed in 1982. However, an Environment Agency project called Thames Estuary 2010 will install new flood walls along the river and many other flood defence techniques to protect the London area against coastal flooding.
● In Bangladesh the Coastal Embankment project has led to the building of 12 sea-facing flood walls and 500 flood shelters.

Figure 3 Houses along the coast of Malibu

ACTIVITIES

Are these statements true? Give reasons for your answer.

● Floods can be predicted with adequate forecasting.
● Floods can be prevented by adequate building design, planning and education.

What are the main types of soft and hard engineering used on the coastline of the UK?

Hard engineering techniques involve major construction work and are usually visually unobtrusive.

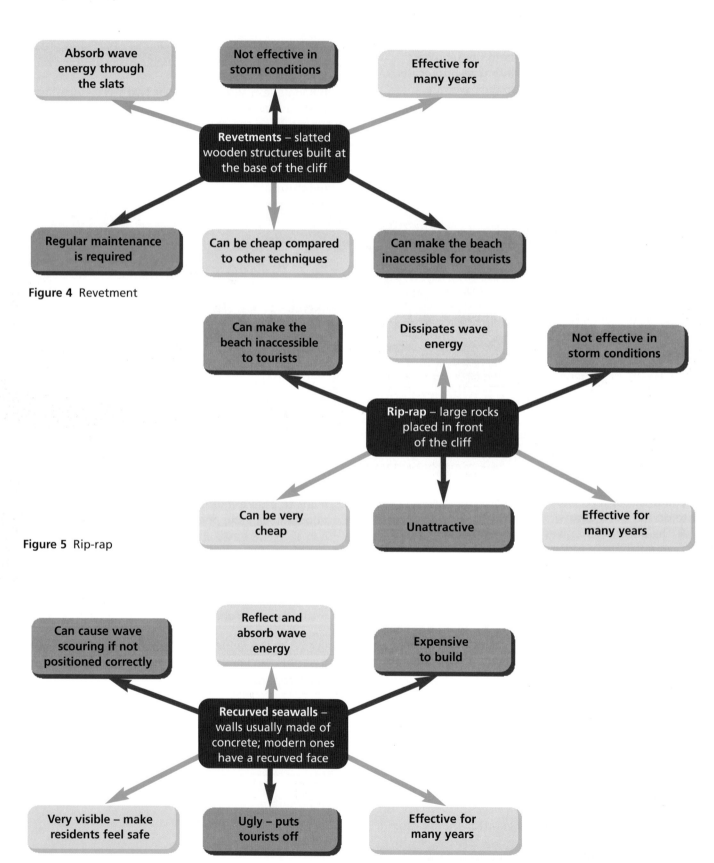

Absorb wave energy through the slats

Not effective in storm conditions

Effective for many years

Revetments – slatted wooden structures built at the base of the cliff

Regular maintenance is required

Can be cheap compared to other techniques

Can make the beach inaccessible for tourists

Figure 4 Revetment

Can make the beach inaccessible to tourists

Dissipates wave energy

Not effective in storm conditions

Rip-rap – large rocks placed in front of the cliff

Can be very cheap

Unattractive

Effective for many years

Figure 5 Rip-rap

Can cause wave scouring if not positioned correctly

Reflect and absorb wave energy

Expensive to build

Recurved seawalls – walls usually made of concrete; modern ones have a recurved face

Very visible – make residents feel safe

Ugly – puts tourists off

Effective for many years

Figure 6 Recurved seawall

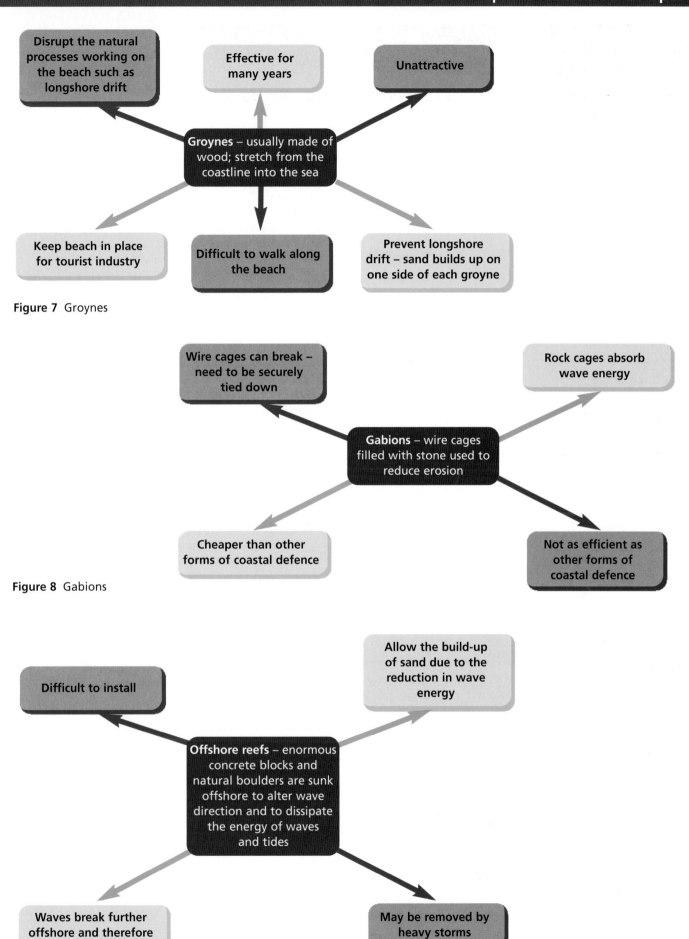

Disrupt the natural processes working on the beach such as longshore drift

Effective for many years

Unattractive

Groynes – usually made of wood; stretch from the coastline into the sea

Keep beach in place for tourist industry

Difficult to walk along the beach

Prevent longshore drift – sand builds up on one side of each groyne

Figure 7 Groynes

Wire cages can break – need to be securely tied down

Rock cages absorb wave energy

Gabions – wire cages filled with stone used to reduce erosion

Cheaper than other forms of coastal defence

Not as efficient as other forms of coastal defence

Figure 8 Gabions

Difficult to install

Allow the build-up of sand due to the reduction in wave energy

Offshore reefs – enormous concrete blocks and natural boulders are sunk offshore to alter wave direction and to dissipate the energy of waves and tides

Waves break further offshore and therefore reduce their erosive power

May be removed by heavy storms

Figure 9 Offshore reefs

The features of soft engineering techniques:

- try to work with the natural processes at work on the coastline
- try to be visually unobtrusive
- do not involve major construction work.

Soft engineering technique	Description	Advantages	Disadvantages
Beach replenishment	The placing of sand and pebbles on a beach.	• Looks natural. • Provides beach for tourists. • A beach is the best form of natural defence because it dissipates wave energy. • Cheap.	• May affect plant and animal life in the area. • The scheme requires constant maintenance; it can all be washed away very quickly in as little as a year. • Disruption for homeowners; large noisy lorries full of sand regularly replenish the beach.
Cliff regrading	The cliff is cut back and given a new gentle slope to stop it slumping.	• May be covered in ecomatting to encourage vegetation growth. • Very natural – will encourage wildlife in the area.	• Not effective alone – needs other defences at the cliff foot. • Some homes on the cliff may have to be demolished.
Managed retreat	Allowing the sea to gradually flood land or erode cliffs.	• Creates new habitats for plants and birds. • Cheap.	• Upsetting for landowners who lose land. • Difficult to estimate the extent of sea movement especially with rising sea levels.

Figure 10 Soft engineering techniques

ACTIVITIES

1 What is the difference between hard and soft engineering techniques?
2 State two disadvantages and two advantages of hard engineering.
3 State two disadvantages and two advantages of soft engineering.

Exam Tip

If you are asked to explain the management of an area, you must state why that particular technique was used.

Coastal management

How is the coast managed in a named location?

You need to be able to describe and explain how the coast is managed at Walton-on-the-Naze.

In 1998, 300 tonnes of Leicester granite were placed around the Tower breakwater which is particularly vulnerable to erosion.

Breakwater built in 1977 to stop longshore drift movement from south to north. It is a wooden structure filled with rip-rap.

In 1999 the beach here was replenished with sand and gravel from Harwich Harbour. Much of this has now been removed due to the longshore drift occurring on this coastline.

Cliff regraded and drainage channels installed in 1977 to produce a gentle more stable slope. The slope was planted with gorse and nettles to stop people climbing on the cliff.

Groyne built in 1977 to stop longshore drift movement from south to north.

Holes in the concrete slabs of the seawall allow rainwater to flow into the sea and not build up in the cliff causing slumping.

Seawall built in 1977 to protect the soft London clay at the bottom of the cliff.

Figure 11 Examples of groynes at Walton-on-the-Naze

Exam Tip

ACTIVITIES

1 Which of the information in Figure 11 is specific?
2 How would you explain why groynes were used to defend Walton?

Hint! Read the information in the text boxes. In one colour highlight the descriptive comments. Use a second colour to highlight the explanation.

Foundation Tier
● Unit 2 Foundation Tier case study questions will sometimes be point marked.
● Full marks cannot be achieved without a specific point and an explanation.

Higher Tier
● **Level 1 (1–2)** A basic answer which has simple descriptive statements.
● **Level 2 (3–4)** A clear answer with level two being reached by there being an explanation or a specific point. The top of the level requires a range of specific points or a number of explanations or a specific point and an explanation.
● **Level 3 (5–6)** An explicit answer with a range of specific and explained points.

River processes produce distinctive landforms

The drainage basin and characteristics of a river and its valley

Middle course
Lateral erosion
Medium gradient
U-shaped valley
Wider river channel
Deeper river channel
Faster flowing
More discharge
Smaller material

Upper course
Vertical erosion
Steep gradient
V-shaped valley
Narrow river channel
Shallow river
Slow flowing (because of friction)
Small discharge
Large rocks

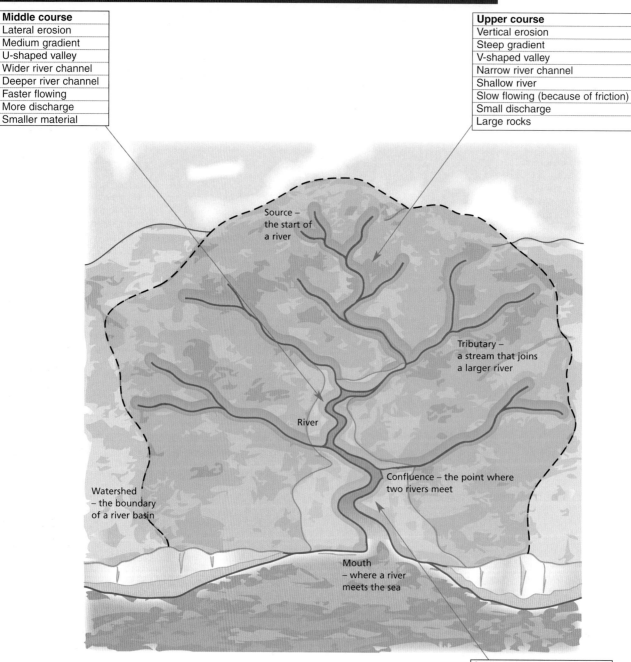

Source – the start of a river

Tributary – a stream that joins a larger river

River

Confluence – the point where two rivers meet

Watershed – the boundary of a river basin

Mouth – where a river meets the sea

Lower course
Mostly deposition
Gentle gradient
Very broad valley
Wider river channel
Deepest river channel
Fastest flowing
Large discharge
Silt and suspended material

Figure 1 Characteristics of a river and its valley

The processes occurring in rivers

The following are processes that are happening in rivers:

Hydraulic action – this is the pressure of the water being pushed against the banks and bed of the river. It also includes the compression of air: as the water gets into cracks in the rock, it compresses the air; this puts even more pressure on the cracks and pieces of rock may break off.

Corrasion – particles (the load) carried by the river are thrown against the river banks with considerable force.

Corrosion (solution) – this is a chemical reaction between certain rock types and the river water.

Attrition – this is a slightly different process that involves the wearing away of the rocks which are in the river. In the upper course of a river rocks continually roll around and knock into each other. They chip away at each other until smooth pebbles or sand are formed.

Deposition – this is the laying down of the load of the river.

What are the main types of weathering?

Physical weathering: freeze–thaw action

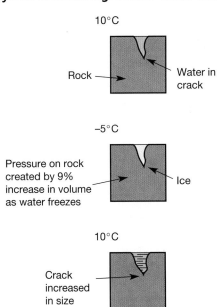

Biological weathering

Seed falls into crack
↓
Rain causes seedling to grow
↓
Roots force their way into cracks
↓
As the roots grow they break up the rock

Burrowing animals also break up rock.

Chemical weathering

Rainwater contains natural acids.

Carbonates in limestone are dissolved by weak acids

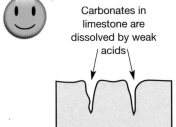

Cracks in rock expand

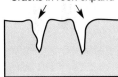

Figure 2 Main types of weathering

What is mass movement?

Mass movement – when material moves down a slope, pulled by gravity

Soil creep
- Slowest downhill movement.
- Gravity pulls water in the soil downhill.
- Soil particles move with the water.
- Heavy rainfall causes faster downhill movement.
- The slope appears to have ripples.
- The ripples are known as terracettes.

Slumping
- This is common on river banks.
- A large area of land moves down the slope.
- This is common on clay river banks.
- During dry weather the clay contracts and cracks.
- When it rains the water runs into the cracks and is absorbed.
- The rock becomes saturated.
- This weakens the rock and, due to the pull of gravity.
- It slips down the slope on the slip plane.

What landforms can be found in river valleys?

The interaction of erosion and deposition has formed a number of distinctive river landforms in the different sections of the river's course: the upper course, the middle course and the lower course.

Waterfall formation

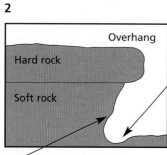

1

Hard rock

Soft rock

2

Hard rock

Soft rock

Overhang

Soft rock eroded back more quickly (by splash back) caused by hydraulic action

Plunge pool formed by the force of the water. It is deepened by the process of corrasion as sediment being carried by the water is scraped against the bottom and sides.

3

Overhang has fallen due to lack of support and pull of gravity

Hard rock

Soft rock

Waterfall retreats upstream to leave a gorge

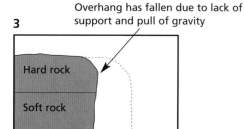

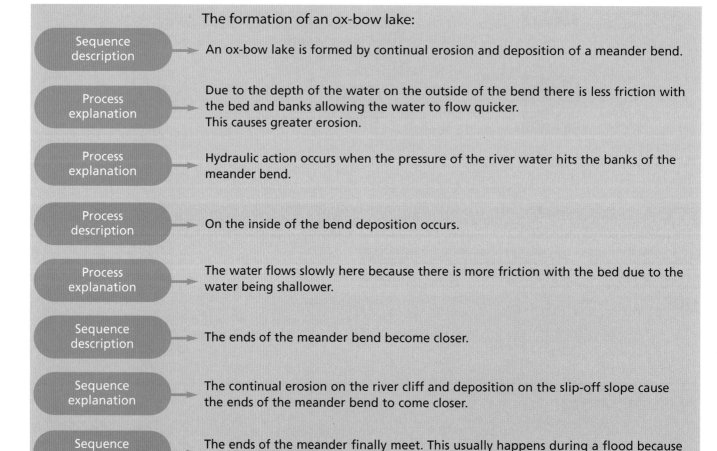

The formation of an ox-bow lake:

Sequence description → An ox-bow lake is formed by continual erosion and deposition of a meander bend.

Process explanation → Due to the depth of the water on the outside of the bend there is less friction with the bed and banks allowing the water to flow quicker.
This causes greater erosion.

Process explanation → Hydraulic action occurs when the pressure of the river water hits the banks of the meander bend.

Process description → On the inside of the bend deposition occurs.

Process explanation → The water flows slowly here because there is more friction with the bed due to the water being shallower.

Sequence description → The ends of the meander bend become closer.

Sequence explanation → The continual erosion on the river cliff and deposition on the slip-off slope cause the ends of the meander bend to come closer.

Sequence explanation → The ends of the meander finally meet. This usually happens during a flood because of the extra power of the water.

Interlocking spurs

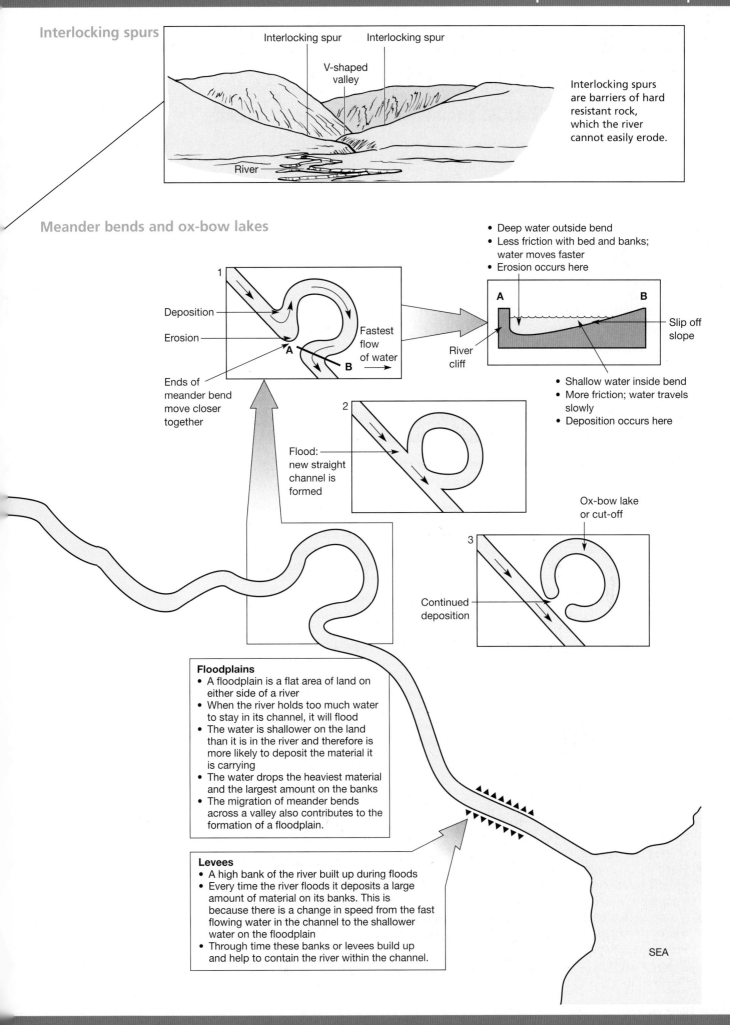

Interlocking spur

Interlocking spur

V-shaped valley

River

Interlocking spurs are barriers of hard resistant rock, which the river cannot easily erode.

Meander bends and ox-bow lakes

1

Deposition

Erosion

Ends of meander bend move closer together

Fastest flow of water

A

B

- Deep water outside bend
- Less friction with bed and banks; water moves faster
- Erosion occurs here

A

B

River cliff

Slip off slope

- Shallow water inside bend
- More friction; water travels slowly
- Deposition occurs here

2

Flood: new straight channel is formed

Ox-bow lake or cut-off

3

Continued deposition

Floodplains
- A floodplain is a flat area of land on either side of a river
- When the river holds too much water to stay in its channel, it will flood
- The water is shallower on the land than it is in the river and therefore is more likely to deposit the material it is carrying
- The water drops the heaviest material and the largest amount on the banks
- The migration of meander bends across a valley also contributes to the formation of a floodplain.

Levees
- A high bank of the river built up during floods
- Every time the river floods it deposits a large amount of material on its banks. This is because there is a change in speed from the fast flowing water in the channel to the shallower water on the floodplain
- Through time these banks or levees build up and help to contain the river within the channel.

SEA

ACTIVITY

Explain the formation of a waterfall. After you have completed your answer, underline the process explanation in one colour and the sequence explanation in another.

For questions about the formation of physical land forms, you will be marked as follows:
- **Foundation Tier** – Maximum three marks for descriptive points; explanations will be credited with one mark. A sequence will be required for maximum marks.
- **Higher Tier** – Maximum two marks for descriptive points; explanations will be credited with one mark each, with a maximum of three marks without a process being mentioned. Full sequence will be required for maximum marks.

Flooding and flood prevention

What are the human and physical causes of river flooding?

Flooding occurs when a river gets more water than its channel can hold. There are both physical and human causes of flooding.

Physical causes of flooding
- If there are large amounts of rain day after day, the water will saturate the ground and flow more quickly into the river.
- During a cloudburst in a thunderstorm, the rain droplets are so large and fall so quickly that there is no time for the water to sink into the ground. Water runs very quickly into the river and causes flooding.
- If there is a sudden rise in temperature, a rapid thaw can happen. Rivers are unable to cope with the amount of water and flood.
- Impermeable rocks mean that rainwater cannot soak into the rocks and it therefore flows more quickly to the river either through the soil or over the surface.
- Steep valley slopes make rainwater run off rapidly into the river channel.
- A long period of hot dry weather makes the soil very hard so that water cannot soak in when it rains. Therefore it runs off the surface into the river.

Human causes of flooding
- If vegetation has been removed, then there is less interception and water will move to the river more quickly.
- Similarly, if there is a town on a floodplain, storm drains will allow water to move into the river at a greater speed and so make flooding more likely.
- Ploughing up and down slopes rather than around them channels the rainwater to the river faster.
- Dams may burst which will cause excess water in river channels and flooding of large areas.

What are the effects of river flooding on people and the environment?

The effects of river flooding on people and the environment should be studied through a range of examples.

Mexico 2007
The River Grijaiva flooded in the state of Tabasco.
- Approximately one million people were affected by the flood.
- 70% of the state was under water.
- All of the crops were destroyed.
- Tabasco's capital, Villahermosa, was turned into a brown lake with only treetops and roofs visible.
- 300,000 people were trapped in their homes.
- Sandbags were placed around several giant heads carved by the Olmecs, an ancient pre-Columbian people, at Tabasco's La Venta archaeological site.

Kenya 2007
The River Tana burst its banks.
- Much of the town of Garissa was under water, with houses near the river submerged.
- The flood destroyed bridges and made roads impassable, meaning aid drops by plane were the only way to deliver food to the starving population.

India 2008
The Kosi river burst its banks.
- 1600 villages were affected.
- Thousands of people were stranded on rooftops and trees or marooned on thin strips of dry land.
- Fifty-five people were killed.
- The road linking Saharia village to the rest of the hard-hit Saharsa district was completely washed away.

USA 2006
Floods caused problems in a number of states.
- 200,000 people were evacuated from their homes in Pennsylvania because of rising waters on the Susquehanna River.
- A state of emergency was declared across large parts of New Jersey, New York and Pennsylvania states.
- The largest evacuation effort took place in Wilkes-Barre, in Pennsylvania.
- A group of children were ferried out of a tennis camp by raft in Philadelphia.
- Numerous roads and bridges were closed.
- Nine people were killed in eastern USA.

Bolivia 2007
Many rivers burst their banks.
- 340,000 people were estimated to have been affected.
- About 100,000 people were left homeless.
- Roads in Santa Cruz and Beni were blocked by mudslides.
- At least 19 people died as a result of flooding of the Rio Grande, a tributary of the Amazon.

ACTIVITY

Explain the effects of river flooding. Use examples in your answer.

Hint! Try and answer the activity question from memory. Remember to apply the correct mark scheme for your tier.

Exam Tip

- Remember to read the question carefully.
- **Foundation Tier** – For questions that ask for examples, you will be marked as follows: each point will receive a mark. If your answer does not contain a specific point about an example, you will lose one mark.
- **Higher Tier** – For questions that ask for examples, your answer will be marked as follows: if the command word is **outline** or **describe**, these questions will usually be marked out of four marks. Each point will receive a mark. If your answer does not include specific points about an example you will only receive two marks. If examples are asked for and you only give one, you will lose one mark.

How are the effects of river flooding reduced by prediction and prevention?

This should be studied through forecasting, building design, planning and education.

Education
- Governments give advice to the general public via the internet. The advice includes information on how to protect your house.
- On the Environment Agency website there is information on the likelihood of a flood. This will be identified by a system of warning codes: flood watch, flood warning, severe flood warning and all clear. These warning codes give people information on what to expect and how to react. In this way the government is helping to prevent the effects of floods by providing an effective warning system.

Forecasting
- The Met Office predicts (forecasts) the likelihood of a flood. The information gets to householders through weather forecasts and news broadcasts on the TV and radio. It is also on their website.
- If there is a likelihood of flooding the Met Office advises householders to be proactive and either ring a flood hotline number or go to the Environment Agency's website to check the likelihood of a flood in their area.

Building design
It can cost between £3000 and £10,000 to protect a house from flooding. Some of the techniques are:
- Moving electricity sockets higher up the walls.
- Replacing doors with ones that are lightweight and can be moved upstairs if necessary.
- Concrete floors instead of wooden ones so they do not rot if they are wet.
- Using yacht varnish on wooden skirting boards to protect them from water.
- Waterproof MDF can also be used instead of wood as a door frame.
- Buildings on stilts.

Planning
- Before houses can be built the local authority has to give planning permission. This is not granted in flood-risk areas unless a flood-risk assessment has been carried out.
- In 2010 the law requires all new housing in flood-risk areas to be flood resistant or resilient.
- Defra (Department for Environment, Food and Rural Affairs) has the responsibility for deciding which areas are going to be defended against the risk of flooding. The Environment Agency then organises for the defences to be built and maintained. Defra provides the money for most of the work that is completed.

ACTIVITIES

Are these statements true? Give reasons for your answer.
- Floods can be predicted with adequate forecasting.
- Floods can be prevented by adequate building design, planning and education.

What are the advantages and disadvantages of soft and hard engineering techniques used to control rivers in the UK?

Hard engineering techniques involve major construction work and are usually visually unobtrusive.

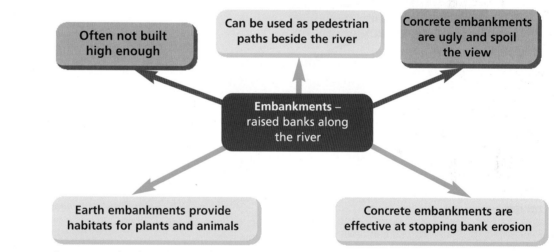

Extremely expensive

No disruption is caused to residents next to the original course of the river

Requires a large amount of land which might be difficult to purchase particularly if it is productive farmland

Flood relief channel – the channel course of the river can also be altered, diverting floodwaters away from settlements

Makes the people who live close to the main river safer as the flood water is diverted into the relief channel

Can be used for water sports

Very effective, should last for many years

Figure 3 Flood relief channels

Often not built high enough

Can be used as pedestrian paths beside the river

Concrete embankments are ugly and spoil the view

Embankments – raised banks along the river

Earth embankments provide habitats for plants and animals

Concrete embankments are effective at stopping bank erosion

Figure 4 Embankments

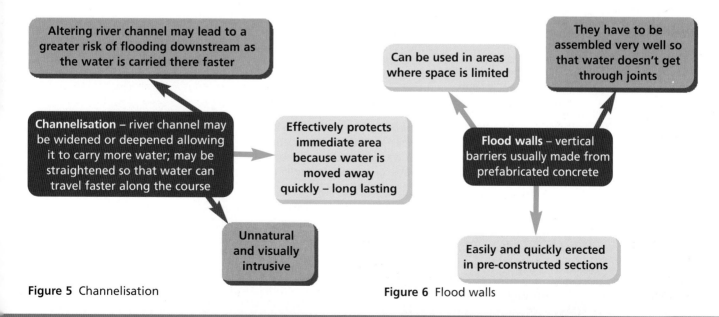

Altering river channel may lead to a greater risk of flooding downstream as the water is carried there faster

Channelisation – river channel may be widened or deepened allowing it to carry more water; may be straightened so that water can travel faster along the course

Effectively protects immediate area because water is moved away quickly – long lasting

Unnatural and visually intrusive

Figure 5 Channelisation

Can be used in areas where space is limited

They have to be assembled very well so that water doesn't get through joints

Flood walls – vertical barriers usually made from prefabricated concrete

Easily and quickly erected in pre-constructed sections

Figure 6 Flood walls

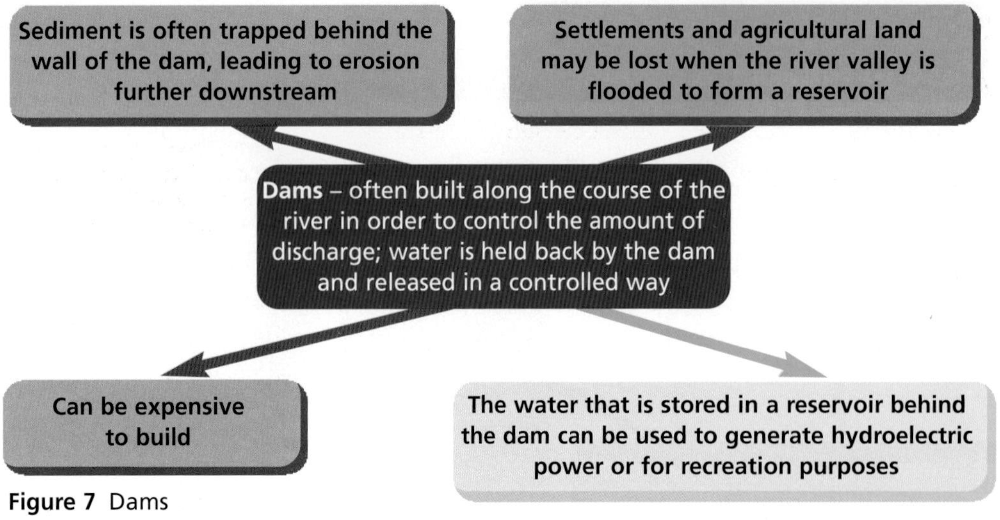

Sediment is often trapped behind the wall of the dam, leading to erosion further downstream

Settlements and agricultural land may be lost when the river valley is flooded to form a reservoir

Dams – often built along the course of the river in order to control the amount of discharge; water is held back by the dam and released in a controlled way

Can be expensive to build

The water that is stored in a reservoir behind the dam can be used to generate hydroelectric power or for recreation purposes

Figure 7 Dams

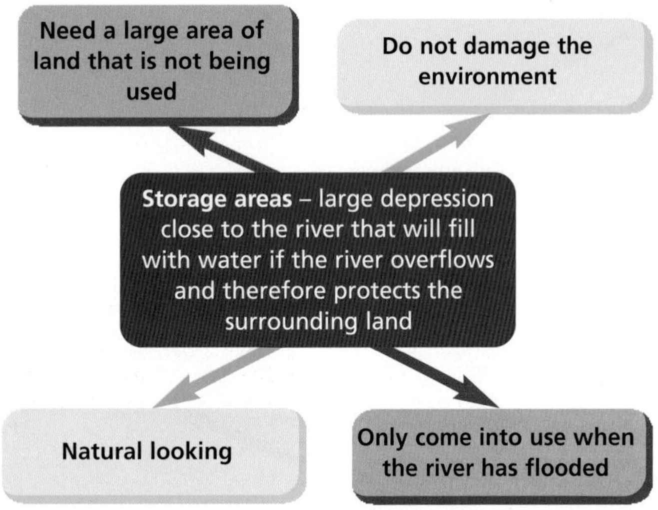

Need a large area of land that is not being used

Do not damage the environment

Storage areas – large depression close to the river that will fill with water if the river overflows and therefore protects the surrounding land

Natural looking

Only come into use when the river has flooded

Figure 8 Storage areas

ACTIVITIES

1 What is the difference between hard and soft engineering techniques?
2 State two disadvantages and two advantages of hard engineering.
3 State two disadvantages and two advantages of soft engineering.

The features of soft engineering techniques:
- try to work with the natural processes at work on the coastline
- try to be visually unobtrusive
- do not involve major construction work.

Soft engineering technique	Description	Advantages	Disadvantages
Floodplain zoning	Local authorities and the national government introduce policies to control urban development close to or on the floodplain.	• Cheap. • Sustainable because it reduces the impact of flooding and building damage is limited. • Because the floodplain hasn't been built on, surface run-off is less likely to cause flooding.	• Resistance to restricting developments in areas where there is a housing shortage. • Enforcing planning regulations and controls may be harder in LICs.
Washlands	The river is allowed to flood naturally in wasteland areas, to prevent flooding in other areas, for example, near settlements.	• Cost-effective as nothing is built. • Provides potential wetlands for birds and plants. • The deposited silt may enrich the soil, turning the area into agricultural land.	• Large areas of land are taken over and cannot be built on. • Productive land can be turned into marshland.
Warning systems	A network of sirens which give people early warning of possible flooding.	• Cheap. • Electronic communication is a very effective way of informing people. • With warning, people can move valuable belongings to a safer place.	• Sirens can be vandalised. • Might not be enough time for residents to prepare.
Afforestation	Trees are planted in the catchment area of the river to intercept the rainfall and slow down the flow of water to the river.	• Relatively low-cost option. • Improves the quality of the environment. • Soil erosion is avoided as trees prevent rapid run-off after heavy rainfall. • Very sustainable.	• It is often conifers that are planted which can make the soil acidic. • Dense tree plantations spoil the natural look of the landscape. • Increases fire risks because of leisure activities in the forest.

Figure 9 Soft engineering techniques

River management

How is a river managed in a named location?

You need to be able to describe and explain how the River Nene has been managed.

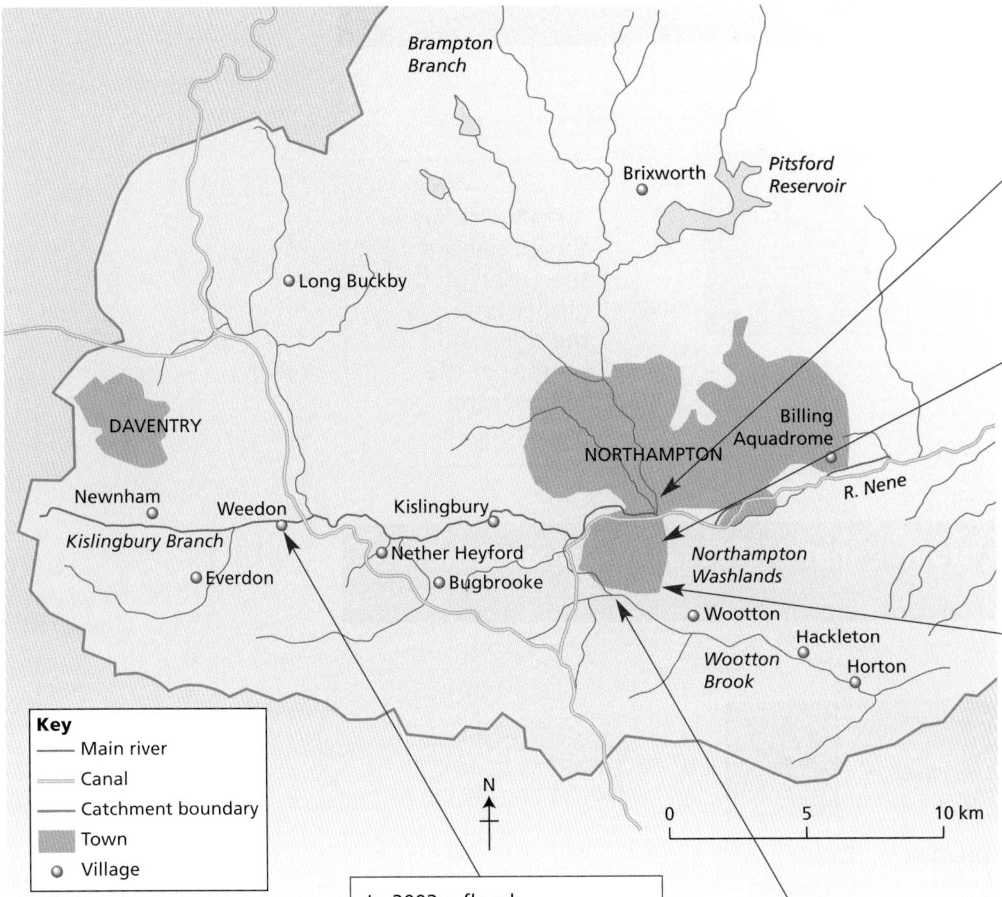

The areas at risk of flooding are covered by the Environment Agency's flood warning service which aims to give 2 hours' notice of the possible onset of flooding. This gives the local people time to prepare and if need be evacuate their house. The flood warning system was upgraded in 2003. Testing of the system took place in the Far Cotton area of Northampton.

At Foot Meadow 4 m high floodwalls have been installed to protect the railway station, housing, industry and the Castle Inn. This has created an open area of land onto which the river can flood.

In 2007 work began to build defences in the Upton area. These defences cost £8 million. The aim of the works is to create an area, called a washland, where up to 1.2 million cubic metres of water can be stored during times of flood.

Major roads in this area such as Upton Way (A45) are on embankments up to 6 m high. This means that communications will not be disrupted even if the river does flood.

In 2002 a flood embankment was built across the river valley at Weedon. This raised the level of the land by 10 m. In times of flood, water can be stored behind the bank.

The river channel capacity at Upton was increased by building earth embankments set back 10 m from the river.

Figure 10 The management of the River Nene

Map labels: Brampton Branch, Brixworth, Pitsford Reservoir, Long Buckby, DAVENTRY, Newnham, Weedon, Kislingbury Branch, Everdon, Kislingbury, Nether Heyford, Bugbrooke, NORTHAMPTON, Billing Aquadrome, R. Nene, Northampton Washlands, Wootton, Wootton Brook, Hackleton, Horton

Key
— Main river
— Canal
— Catchment boundary
▓ Town
○ Village

N

0   5   10 km

ACTIVITY

Which of the information in Figure 10 is specific?

Exam Tip

Hint! Read the information in the text boxes. In one colour highlight the descriptive comments. Use a second colour to highlight the explanation.

Foundation Tier
● Foundation Tier case study questions will sometimes be point marked.
● Full marks cannot be achieved without a specific point and an explanation if asked for.

Higher Tier
● Level 1 (1–2) A basic answer which has simple descriptive statements.
● Level 2 (3–4) A clear answer with level two being reached by there being an explanation or a specific point. The top of the level requires a range of specific points or a number of explanations or a specific point and explanation.
● Level 3 (5–6) An explicit answer with a range of specific and explained points.

The impact of glaciation on river valleys

What are the processes of glacial erosion?

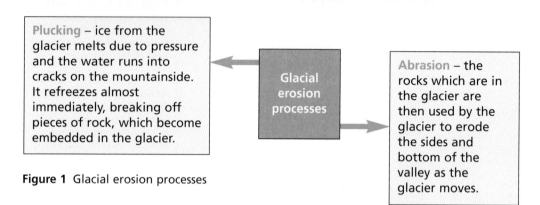

Plucking – ice from the glacier melts due to pressure and the water runs into cracks on the mountainside. It refreezes almost immediately, breaking off pieces of rock, which become embedded in the glacier.

Glacial erosion processes

Abrasion – the rocks which are in the glacier are then used by the glacier to erode the sides and bottom of the valley as the glacier moves.

Figure 1 Glacial erosion processes

How does freeze–thaw provide material for abrasion and the formation of moraines?

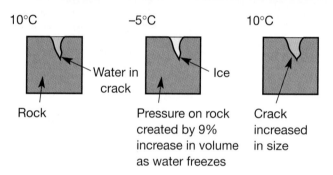

10°C

Rock

–5°C

Water in crack

Pressure on rock created by 9% increase in volume as water freezes

10°C

Ice

Crack increased in size

Figure 2 The process of freeze–thaw

Freeze–thaw only happens when:

- temperatures vary above and below zero
- water is present
- there are cracks in the rock.

The continual freezing and thawing of the water causes rocks to break up. The broken rock material can then be used by the glacier to erode through the process of abrasion or it is deposited as moraine.

What landforms are found in glaciated uplands?

Corries

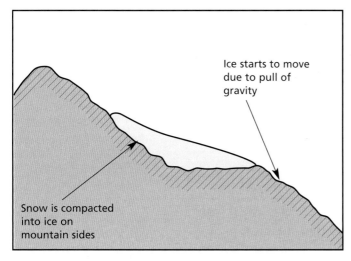

Ice starts to move due to pull of gravity

Snow is compacted into ice on mountain sides

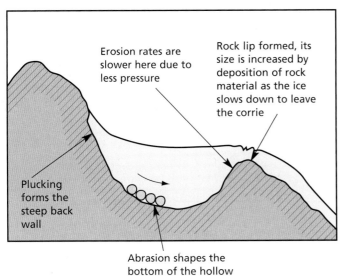

Erosion rates are slower here due to less pressure

Rock lip formed, its size is increased by deposition of rock material as the ice slows down to leave the corrie

Plucking forms the steep back wall

Abrasion shapes the bottom of the hollow

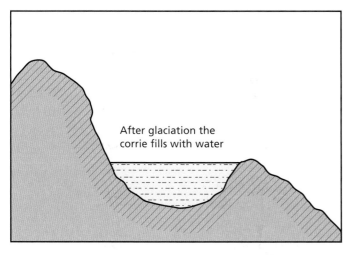

After glaciation the corrie fills with water

The formation of a corrie:

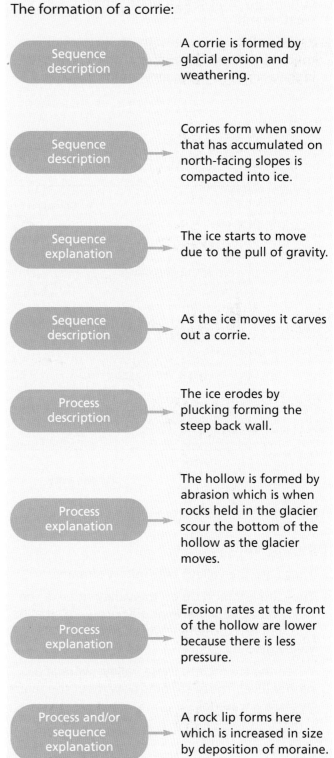

Sequence description → A corrie is formed by glacial erosion and weathering.

Sequence description → Corries form when snow that has accumulated on north-facing slopes is compacted into ice.

Sequence explanation → The ice starts to move due to the pull of gravity.

Sequence description → As the ice moves it carves out a corrie.

Process description → The ice erodes by plucking forming the steep back wall.

Process explanation → The hollow is formed by abrasion which is when rocks held in the glacier scour the bottom of the hollow as the glacier moves.

Process explanation → Erosion rates at the front of the hollow are lower because there is less pressure.

Process and/or sequence explanation → A rock lip forms here which is increased in size by deposition of moraine.

Arêtes and pyramidal peaks

- If two corries form beside each other on a mountainside their sides will become knife-edge ridges known as arêtes. These are continually attacked by freeze–thaw weathering.

- If corries form on at least three sides of a mountain the top becomes a sharp peak of jagged rock known as a pyramidal peak.

Ribbon lakes

- These are long narrow lakes in valleys in upland areas that have been glaciated.

- They were formed when the glacier met less resistant rock on the valley floor and eroded more here to form a dip in the valley bottom.

- After glaciation this filled with water.

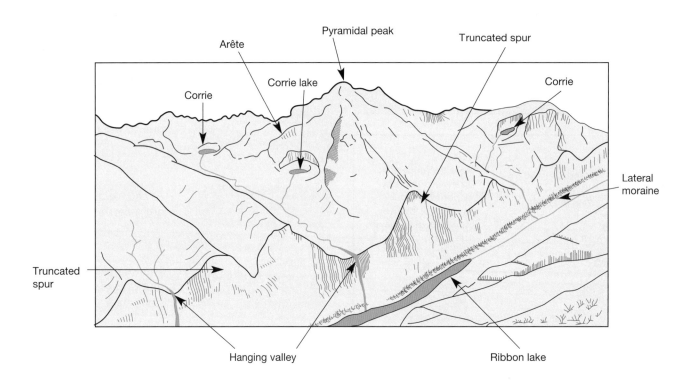

Hanging valleys

- These are the valleys of tributary streams.

- They are left high up on the valley sides of the main valley because their glaciers were smaller and had less erosive power than the main valley glaciers.

- When the ice melted these valleys were at a higher level. These streams now meet the main river via a waterfall.

U-shaped valleys and truncated spurs

- A valley glacier will completely fill a river valley. It has a lot of power to erode because of its size and weight.

- This great power cuts back the interlocking spurs using abrasion and plucking, forming truncated spurs.

- This leaves a wide flat-bottomed valley with steep cliff-like sides.

Before glaciation

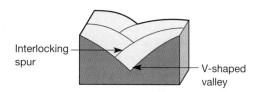

Interlocking spur

V-shaped valley

After glaciation

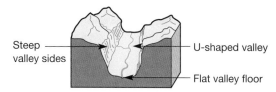

Steep valley sides

U-shaped valley

Flat valley floor

Figure 3 A valley before and after glaciation

The diagrams show the same valley before and after glaciation.

ACTIVITY

Explain the formation of a U-shaped valley. After you have completed your answer, underline the process explanation in one colour and the sequence explanation in another.

Remember! When answering a question on landform formation:
- Sequence
- Process
- Explain
- Describe.

Exam Tip

For questions that ask about the formation of the physical landforms, you will be marked as follows:

- **Foundation Tier** – Maximum three marks for descriptive points; explanations credited at one mark. A sequence will be required for maximum marks.

- **Higher Tier** – Maximum two marks for descriptive points; explanations credited with one mark each, with a maximum of three marks without a process being mentioned. Full sequence will be required for maximum marks.

What are the processes of glacial deposition?

There are two processes by which a glacier deposits material.

1 **Lodgement** – this is material that is deposited by a glacier. The glacier becomes so full of debris that it does not have the energy to carry it. It also occurs due to an increase in ice thickness causing friction between the glacier and the ground. Material in the glacier will be spread onto the valley floor.
2 **Ablation** – this is where material is deposited as the ice melts. For example, in the summer the glacier will melt and retreat leaving material deposited along its valley.

What landforms are created by glacial deposition?

Moraine

- This is material transported and deposited by glaciers.
- There are four types of moraine.
- Moraine is collected by the glacier from freeze–thaw weathering, plucking and abrasion.
- Moraine will be dropped where the glacier slows down.
- Lateral moraine is dropped at the sides of glaciers.
- Ground moraine is put down below the glacier.
- Where two glaciers meet their lateral moraines become medial moraines.
- Terminal moraine is dropped where the glacier ends.

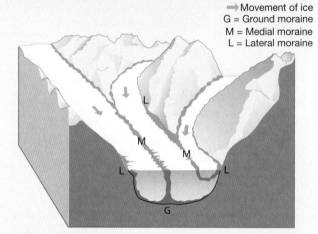

Movement of ice
G = Ground moraine
M = Medial moraine
L = Lateral moraine

Figure 4 Moraine

Drumlins

Drumlins are small egg-shaped hills, typically 10–50 m high with the steeper slope and highest point at the end facing the ice. They are usually found in groups or 'swarms'.

Drumlins are formed when the power of the glacier is reduced. This causes the material that is being carried by the glacier to be deposited. The reasons for the power of the glacier being reduced could be because of:

- the ice melting
- the ice moving slower
- an obstacle such as a rock outcrop interrupting the flow.

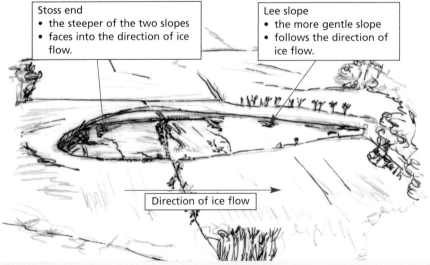

Stoss end
- the steeper of the two slopes
- faces into the direction of ice flow.

Lee slope
- the more gentle slope
- follows the direction of ice flow.

Direction of ice flow

Figure 5 A field sketch of a drumlin

Erratics

Erratics are pieces of rock that vary in size from small pebbles to large boulders. They have been transported and deposited into an area of differing rock type – they are geologically out of place. An example is the blue granite blocks in Lancashire that are unique to Ailsa Crag, an island off the Ayrshire coast. This shows that the ice sheet that deposited them moved 240 km in a south-west direction.

How people use glaciated landscapes

How do people use glaciated landscapes?

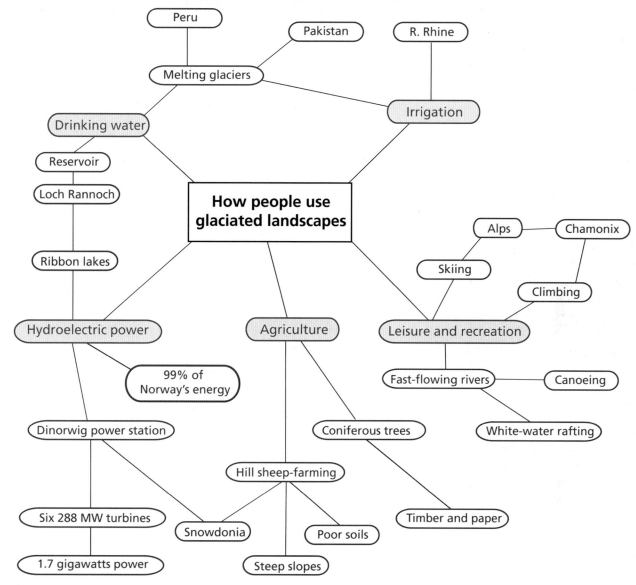

Figure 6 Human uses of glaciated areas

ACTIVITY

Try and answer the following from memory:
Outline how people use glaciated landscapes. Use examples in your answer.

Exam Tip

● **Foundation Tier** – For questions that ask for examples, your answer will be marked as follows:
Each point will receive a mark. If your answer does not contain a specific point about an example you will lose one mark.

● **Higher Tier** – If the command word is **outline** or **describe**, these questions will usually be marked out of four marks. Each point will receive a mark. If your answer does not include specific points about an example you will only receive two marks. If examples are asked for and you only give one you will lose one mark.

Avalanches and their management

What were the physical and human causes and effects of the Galtür avalanche on 23 February 1999?

Figure 7 Avalanche!

What were the physical causes?

- A complex weather system led to the avalanche. On 20 January, an Atlantic storm formed 4000 km away. As the storm moved north it cooled forming a system of fronts with towering clouds.
- This caused 4 m of snow to fall in the Galtür area in February, breaking all records.
- Galtür also had almost 3 weeks of very strong winds up to 100 km/hour. This caused massive accumulations of snow. If the wind had come from a different direction then the snow would have drifted onto the slopes facing away from the village, but the strong north-west winds blew towards Galtür.
- More snow than usual built up on top of a weak layer of snow. The weak layer could no longer hold up the weight of the overlying snow and it finally gave way. An 800 m section of snow travelled down the mountain at 200 km/hour. In 6 seconds it hit the village of Galtür.

What were the human causes?

- There was a lack of avalanche protection schemes as they weren't thought necessary in the Wasser-Leiter area.

What were the effects of the avalanche on the environment?

- Only a little damage was done to the environment as the path of the avalanche was mostly over open terrain.
- Some trees were destroyed which had a minor effect on the animal habitats.

What were the effects of the avalanche on people?

- Thirty-one people died: 26 tourists and five locals.
- Eleven people severely injured.
- Six people required intensive care at the hospital in Landeck.
- Over 30,000 people were evacuated from the area.
- All roads closed for 4 days.
- Tour operators cancelled holiday bookings causing a loss of earnings for hotels and other tourist facilities.
- Ski resorts along the Paznaun Valley were closed costing them £5 million a day in lost revenue.
- Four local houses completely destroyed, one of which had its roof chopped off by a slab of ice.
- Twelve buildings were severely damaged.
- Forty other buildings were buried beneath the snow but remained intact.
- All roads closed for 4 days.
- Rescue equipment was buried at the fire station of Galtür. It took 2 days to dig it out.
- One hundred cars were smashed.
- There was approximately £7.5 million damage done to property.

Exam Tip

- **Foundation Tier** – Case study questions will sometimes be point marked. Full marks cannot be achieved without a specific point and an explanation if asked for.
- **Higher Tier**
  Level 1 (1–2) A basic answer which has simple descriptive statements.
  Level 2 (3–4) A clear answer with level two being reached by there being an explanation or a specific point. The top of the level requires a range of specific points or a number of explanations or a specific point and an explanation.
  Level 3 (5–6) An explicit answer with a range of specific and explained points.

How the effects of avalanches are reduced by prediction and prevention

Forecasting

- Predictions are made by experienced avalanche forecasters. They collect samples of snow to analyse current weather data and past conditions to make predictions.
- Then avalanche warnings are prepared at ski resorts.
- The risk of an avalanche is assessed on a five-level scale: 1 is low risk, 5 very high risk.
- Coloured flags are also used. Yellow is low risk, chequered is high risk and black is very high risk.

Planning and education

- 'No build areas' are set up in mountain settlements susceptible to avalanches. In Austria settlements in avalanche areas are zoned according to risk. In red zones construction of any kind is prohibited. In yellow zones safety measures and strict building codes are enforced so that if struck by an avalanche the buildings will withstand the force and people should not be harmed.
- Skiers are informed of the risks by flags and information posted in ski resorts.
- Areas more likely to suffer avalanches are cordoned off to skiers.
- Controlled avalanches are set off to prevent larger more powerful uncontrolled avalanches.
- Ski rangers and patrol teams test areas before opening them to the public.

Design of buildings

- New buildings in avalanche zones are to be avalanche proof. Buildings have reinforced concrete walls; they are shaped to deflect the avalanche; no windows are built facing the approaching avalanche to limit damage by shattered glass.

ACTIVITIES

1 Outline the defences that are used in mountainous areas to protect people from avalanches.
2 Are these statements true? Give reasons for your answer.
  - Avalanches can be predicted with adequate forecasting.
  - Avalanches can be prevented by adequate building design, planning and education.

Trees act as a useful barrier to stop, slow down or break the flow of an avalanche.

Snow fences help to stabilise the snow. They can be made of natural wood, or metal which looks more ugly but is stronger.

Snow shed protecting the access road. A concrete roof is built over the road and supported by concrete pillars. The gaps provide better visibility for motorists.

Figure 8 Some avalanche protection schemes

Location and characteristics of tectonic activity

The world's distribution of earthquakes and volcanoes

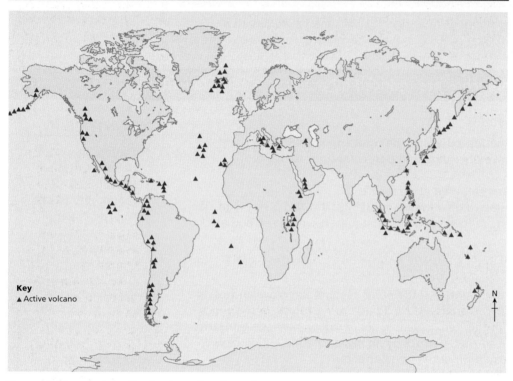

Key
▲ Active volcano

N

Figure 1 The world's distribution of active volcanoes

Exam Tip

How to answer a question on distribution
Question: Describe the distribution of volcanoes in Figure 1.
Possible answer: Many volcanoes are found around the Pacific Ocean. There is a line of volcanoes running down the middle of the Atlantic Ocean. There are no volcanoes in Australia. Volcanoes are found both on land and sea. Nearly all the volcanoes on the land are sited close to the oceans.

Note the similarity between the plate boundaries and the distribution of volcanoes. Volcanoes are found at convergent and divergent boundaries, but not at conservative boundaries.

For distribution questions write down what you see.

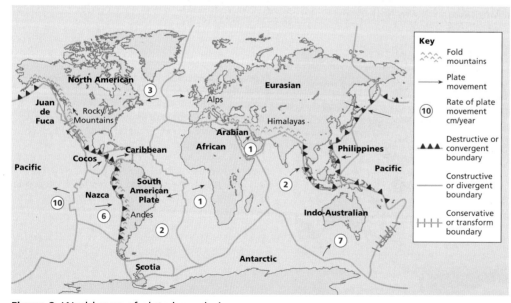

Key

~~~ Fold mountains

→ Plate movement

⑩ Rate of plate movement cm/year

▲▲▲ Destructive or convergent boundary

— Constructive or divergent boundary

╫╫╫ Conservative or transform boundary

North American, Juan de Fuca, Rocky Mountains, Alps, Eurasian, Himalayas, Arabian, African, Philippines, Caribbean, Cocos, Pacific, Pacific, South American Plate, Nazca, Andes, Indo-Australian, Scotia, Antarctic

Figure 2 World map of plate boundaries

You will not gain extra marks for explanations.

This also applies to the distribution of earthquakes.

Reasons why earthquakes and volcanoes occur where they do

What is plate tectonics?

This is a theory that explains why earthquakes and volcanoes are found where they are.

- The Earth's crust is divided into seven large and 13 smaller plates.
- Plates move a few centimetres a year.
- They float on the molten mantle.
- Convection currents in the mantle cause the plates to move.
- Plate movement causes continents to collide, and split apart.
- The changing position of the continents is called continental drift.
- The plate boundaries are under extreme pressure and this is where most of the Earth's earthquakes and volcanoes occur.

What are hotspots?

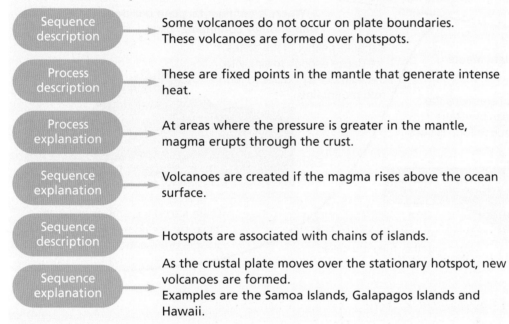

Sequence description → Some volcanoes do not occur on plate boundaries. These volcanoes are formed over hotspots.

Process description → These are fixed points in the mantle that generate intense heat.

Process explanation → At areas where the pressure is greater in the mantle, magma erupts through the crust.

Sequence explanation → Volcanoes are created if the magma rises above the ocean surface.

Sequence description → Hotspots are associated with chains of islands.

Sequence explanation → As the crustal plate moves over the stationary hotspot, new volcanoes are formed.
Examples are the Samoa Islands, Galapagos Islands and Hawaii.

Characteristics of plate boundaries

The Earth's crust is made up of several tectonic plates. Convection currents in the molten area beneath the crust called the mantle cause the plates to move. **Movement has the greatest impact at plate boundaries where two plates meet.**

There are three different types of plate movement:

- Some plates move towards each other (converge). This is called a **convergent plate boundary.**
- Some plates move away from each other (diverge). This is called a **divergent plate boundary.**
- Some plates move alongside each other. This is called a **conservative plate boundary.**

Convergent plate boundaries

Convergent plate boundaries are split into three types:

1 Where an oceanic plate collides with a continental plate

The denser oceanic plate is forced beneath the continental plate.

A deep ocean trench is produced where the oceanic plate starts to subduct

Powerful earthquakes occur as the plates move

Fold mountains form as the land is buckled.

Ocean

Direction of plate movement

The oceanic plate melts under the continental crust

Direction of plate movement

This molten rock (magma) forces its way upwards and erupts as volcanoes.

Exam Tip

These diagrams are simple ones that you could easily sketch in an exam. They would help any answer on plate boundaries. You can still draw diagrams to help your answer even if the question doesn't directly ask for one.

3 Where a continental plate collides with another continental plate

Because neither of the plates are dense enough to sink into the mantle they buckle to form **fold mountains**

2 Where an oceanic plate meets another oceanic plate

After several eruptions the volcanoes can break the ocean surface to form islands

Deep ocean trench

Ocean

Earthquakes are common

MANTLE

Volcanic activity and earthquakes both characterise this plate boundary

When several of these islands form together they are called an **island arc**

There are no volcanic eruptions at this plate boundary because no crust is being subducted and melted

MANTLE

Divergent plate boundaries

Undersea volcanoes form mid-ocean ridges

Where volcanoes emerge above the sea, islands are formed, e.g. Iceland

Sea floor spreads new crust is formed

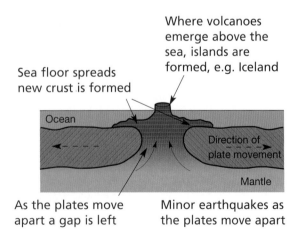

Ocean

Direction of plate movement

Mantle

As the plates move apart a gap is left

Minor earthquakes as the plates move apart

Magma rises from the mantle to fill the gap

Conservative plate boundaries

- Plates move in different directions or at different speeds.
- Plates become locked together.
- Pressure builds until rock snaps along a fault.
- Plates move suddenly causing powerful earthquakes.
- No volcanic eruptions happen here.

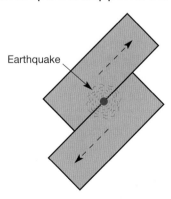

Earthquake

How are earthquakes measured?

Mercalli scale	Richter scale
Measured on a scale of 1–12.	Measured on a scale of 1–9.
Measures the intensity of an earthquake.	Measures the magnitude of an earthquake.
It is an arbitrary scale based on observations of damage to buildings and the environment.	It is a scientific scale based on accurate measurements.
Measured by people.	Measured by a seismograph.
Difficult to measure in an uninhabited area as there will be few, if any visible effects.	Vibrations can be measured anywhere.
You have to be where the earthquake is to measure it.	Do not have to be there.
Difficult to measure intensities of 1–3 because they have little effect on people or the environment.	All scales easy to measure because they are measured by a machine.
Only uses whole numbers.	More specific as each scale is split into 10 points.

The differences between the two scales are shown in the table on the left.

What are the characteristics of the focus and epicentre of an earthquake?

Focus
- A point below the ground.
- The depth below ground can vary.
- Shockwaves radiate out from here.
- Where crustal tension is released.

Epicentre
- A point on the surface.
- Area of greatest destruction.
- Visible sign of earthquake.

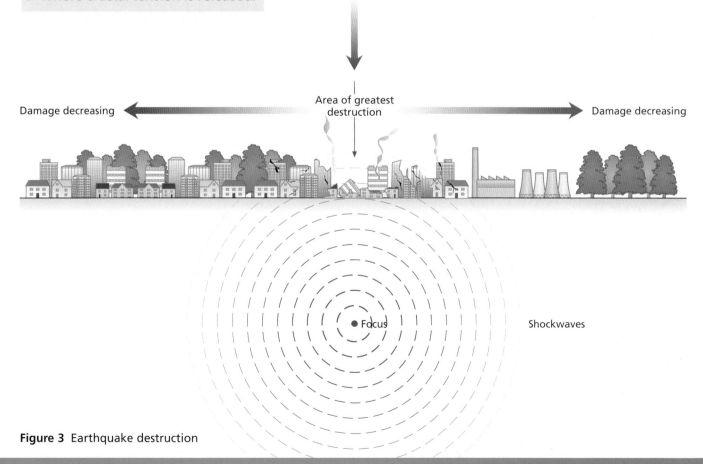

Figure 3 Earthquake destruction

Management of the effects of tectonic activity

Why do people continue to live in areas of volcanic and earthquake activity?

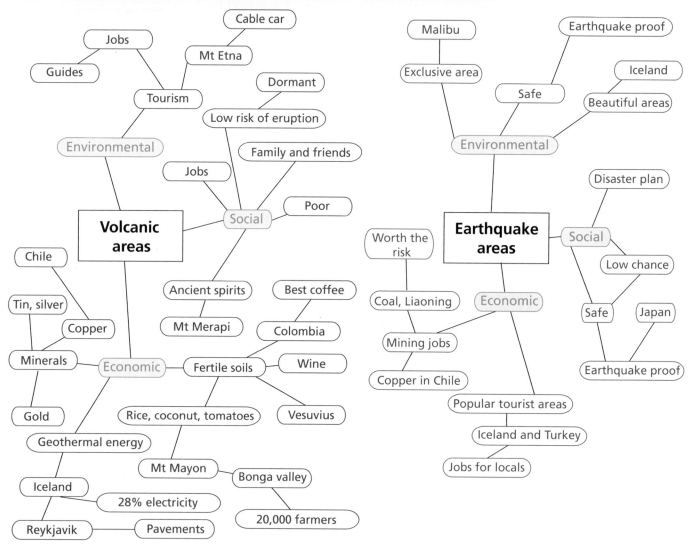

Figure 4 The reasons why people continue to live in areas of volcanic and earthquake activity

ACTIVITY

Explain why people continue to live in areas of volcanic and earthquake activity. Use examples in your answer.

Hint! Try and answer this question from memory. Remember to apply the correct mark scheme for your tier.

The causes and effects of an earthquake in a named location

You need to be able to describe and explain the causes and effects of the earthquake in Turkey in 1999.

Causes

- Turkey is being squeezed between three tectonic plates: Eurasian, African and Arabian.
- This has created numerous faults (cracks in the Earth's surface).
- Izmit is on the North Anatolian fault.
- The North Anatolian fault slipped between 2 and 5 m causing the earthquake.
- The land underneath Izmit is made of soft clay and sand which move easier than solid rock.

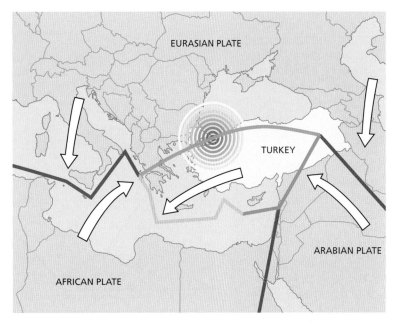

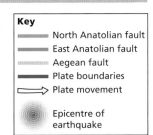

Key

▤▤▤	North Anatolian fault
━━━	East Anatolian fault
┈┈┈	Aegean fault
━━━	Plate boundaries
⟹	Plate movement
◎	Epicentre of earthquake

Effect on environment

- 700,000 tonnes of oil was set on fire at the Tupras oil refinery.
- The toxic waste dump at Petkim was cracked, exposing waste.
- The waste treatment plant at Petkim was damaged leading to raw sewage spilling into the rivers and killing fish.
- A 6 m tidal wave struck Degirmendere causing coastal erosion and damage to the town park.
- There was a chemical leakage from a chlorine factory in Yalova.

Effect on people

- 18,000 people died, most of them due to collapsed buildings.
- 300,000 made homeless. Even 2 years after the quake 20,000 people were still living in temporary accommodation, tents or prefabricated huts.
- In Yalova 65,000 houses destroyed.
- The motorway between Ankara (the capital) and Istanbul (the largest city) buckled leading to cars crashing into each other and causing transport to be disrupted.
- People had psychological problems leading to sleeplessness and withdrawal.
- Rebuilding the affected area cost $10 billion.

ACTIVITIES

Choose either Turkey or Montserrat (see page 36).

1 Construct a table which has columns headed Causes and Effects. Complete the table using one colour for descriptive points and a second colour for explanation.

2 Underline the specific points in your table.

Exam Tip

- **Foundation Tier** – Case study questions will sometimes be point marked. Full marks cannot be achieved without a specific point and an explanation if asked for.
- **Higher Tier**
  Level 1 (1–2) A basic answer which has simple descriptive statements.
  Level 2 (3–4) A clear answer with level two being reached by there being an explanation or a specific point. The top of the level requires a range of specific points or a number of explanations or a specific point and an explanation.
  Level 3 (5–6) An explicit answer with a range of specific and explained points.

The causes and effects of a volcanic eruption in a named location

You need to be able to describe and explain the causes and effects of the volcanic eruption in Montserrat in 1997.

Causes
- The volcanic island of Montserrat is situated on a destructive plate boundary. The North American plate is slowly being forced under (subducted) the Caribbean plate.
- This happens because the oceanic North American plate is denser than the Caribbean continental plate.
- Convection currents pull the dense North American plate into the mantle where intense heat and friction cause the rock to melt. This molten rock is lighter than the surrounding rock, forcing it to rise through cracks in the rock towards the Earth's surface forming the volcanic island of Montserrat.
- On 25 June 1997, at about one o'clock in the afternoon, Chances Peak Volcano on the island of Montserrat erupted catastrophically.

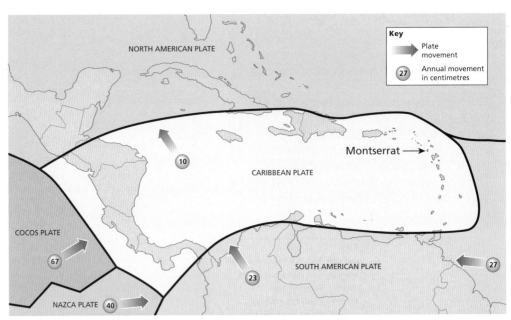

Effects on people
- Some unauthorised people were in the exclusion zone set up in 1995. They were too far away to hear the warning sirens but thought they would receive audible warning from the volcano if it was going to erupt. Unfortunately this didn't happen and many people were caught unawares.
- Nineteen people, mostly farmers, were killed by the pyroclastic flows. The farmers were producing crops to feed evacuees and believed that they were helping their country in crisis. Most land suitable for farming was in the south of the island, close to the volcano.
- Of these 19, seven people were killed by a pyroclastic surge in the Streatham and Windy Hill area, and six of the victims were found outside houses.
- The villages of Farm and Trant were completely buried by ash flow deposits.
- Common injuries were severe burns to the feet as a result of walking on ash deposits. Other survivors suffered burns to various parts of their bodies, including burns to the nose and mouth due to breathing in the hot gases.
- 100–150 houses were destroyed. Houses were partially buried or burned by the intense heat. Aluminium window shutters were melted and twisted. Everything made from wood was burned. Other houses were destroyed by direct impact of rocks, up to 5 m in size.

Effects on environment
- During the eruption 5 million cubic metres of rock and ash were deposited, covering 4 square kilometres of land.
- The pyroclastic flows broke and flattened thousands of trees. In some areas there was no vegetation left at all. Vegetable beds were bare of plants and the soil was baked hard.
- Deposits completely filled Pea Ghaut and formed a thick, broad fan emerging north-west from Paradise River just north of Bethel. Houses up to 200 m from the edge of the fan were completely buried by deposits. Some of the rocks deposited in Bethel were up to 5 m in size. This caused widespread destruction.
- The pyroclastic surges spread out and flattened trees on the ridges surrounding Farrell's Yard.
- The pyroclastic flows extended westwards travelling as far as the last bend in the valley before Cork Hill causing the Belham River to flood.

Prediction and prevention of the effects of volcanic eruptions and earthquakes

Can the effects of earthquakes and volcanic eruptions be limited?

Prediction (forecasting)

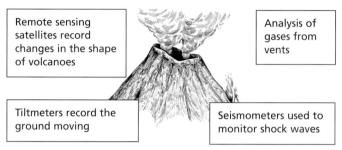

Remote sensing satellites record changes in the shape of volcanoes

Analysis of gases from vents

Tiltmeters record the ground moving

Seismometers used to monitor shock waves

Figure 5 Predicting volcanic eruptions

Building design and defence

The diagram shows a range of techniques that are used to make buildings earthquake proof.

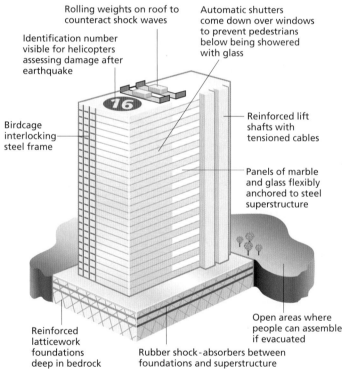

Rolling weights on roof to counteract shock waves

Automatic shutters come down over windows to prevent pedestrians below being showered with glass

Identification number visible for helicopters assessing damage after earthquake

Birdcage interlocking steel frame

Reinforced lift shafts with tensioned cables

Panels of marble and glass flexibly anchored to steel superstructure

Reinforced latticework foundations deep in bedrock

Rubber shock-absorbers between foundations and superstructure

Open areas where people can assemble if evacuated

Figure 6 Earthquake-proof buildings

Planning and education

Emergency drills – Japan have an annual earthquake day where children in schools practise earthquake procedures.

Emergency plans – This is how Californians are told to prepare for an earthquake:

1 have flashlights and batteries ready
2 have first-aid kit and fire extinguisher ready
3 store a few gallons of water per family member
4 store one week's food outside the house
5 place beds away from windows and mirrors
6 agree on a plan to reunite the family by day or night.

Examples of building design
- The Tamaki building in Auckland has been built in two blocks with a 10 cm gap between them to allow a controlled movement which will dissipate the force of an earthquake.
- San Francisco International Airport has 267 columns each resting on a 1.5 m ball-bearing. These allow the building to move as much as 50 cm without causing damage.
- The Basilica at Assisi was destroyed by an earthquake in 1997. When it was rebuilt engineers installed special wires designed to stretch and snap back like elastic to help protect it against future tremors.

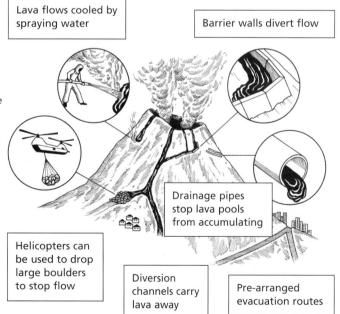

Lava flows cooled by spraying water

Barrier walls divert flow

Drainage pipes stop lava pools from accumulating

Helicopters can be used to drop large boulders to stop flow

Diversion channels carry lava away

Pre-arranged evacuation routes

Figure 7 Volcano damage prevention by defence

ACTIVITIES

Are these statements true? Give reasons for your answer.
- Earthquakes and volcanic activity can be predicted with adequate forecasting.
- Damage caused by earthquakes and volcanic activity can be prevented by adequate building design, planning and education.

5 A Wasteful World

Types of waste and its production

What types of waste are there?

Some of the ways that waste can be categorised:
- biodegradable and non-biodegradable
- domestic and industrial
- hazardous or non-hazardous
- solid or liquid.

What are the differences between HIC and LIC waste production?

ACTIVITY

Study the text on the left about the waste produced by HICs. State why LICs do not produce as much waste as HICs.

HICs contain 20% of the world's population but consume 86% of the world's products. People in HICs have more money and buy more products. This is known as the consumer society. If people have more things they have more to throw away hence more waste!

The table below gives information about the amount of waste produced by countries at different stages of development in 2002.

Country	Waste generated in 2002 (kilograms per person per year)	Stage of development
Bangladesh	17	LIC
Brazil	330	MIC
China	149	MIC
Congo	10	LIC
France	538	HIC
UK	590	HIC

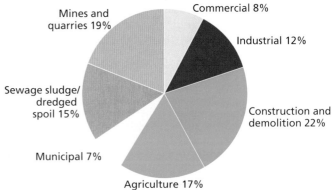

Figure 1 Different types of waste produced in the UK

Most countries in the world will produce the same types of waste but the volume of the different categories will differ dependent on the stage of development of the country.

Figure 1 shows the different types of waste produced in the UK in 2000.

An example of HIC and LIC consumption differences

The city of Los Angeles, USA, produces approximately 1250 kg of rubbish per person each year. This is due to the wealth of the people who live there who consume vast amounts of products and therefore have a lot of waste.

The people in Abidjan, on the Ivory Coast, Africa, only generate 200 kg of rubbish a year! These are poor people without the means to buy many consumer products.

ACTIVITY

How do you think the waste produced in Bangladesh would differ from the waste produced in the UK?

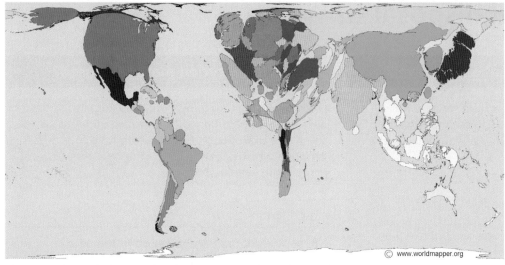

Figure 2 Choropleth map showing waste in selected countries

© www.worldmapper.org

ACTIVITY

Describe the distribution of waste production.
What is the level of development of the countries that produce the most waste?

Exam Tip

- You may be asked to describe a distribution on a map. You should start with general points.
- Your answer should then become more specific naming countries or continents.
- If data is asked for, you will lose a mark if you don't include it.
- If data is not requested you should still include some as you will be given credit.

What types of domestic waste are produced by HICs?

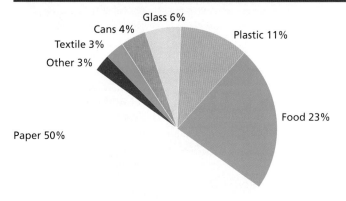

Glass 6%
Cans 4%
Plastic 11%
Textile 3%
Other 3%
Food 23%
Paper 50%

Domestic waste is the waste that is produced by the average household

Figure 3 Types of domestic waste in the USA: a HIC

ACTIVITY

Compare the types of waste produced by the USA and Bangladesh.

Exam Tip

- When the command word **compare** is used, you should state the similarities between the figures. However, examiners at GCSE will also credit comments about the differences (contrasts).
- You do not need to know the types of waste produced by a LIC but it might be used as a comparison.

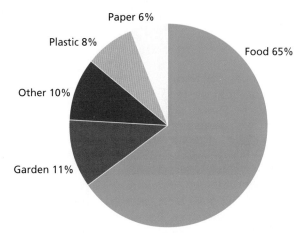

Paper 6%
Plastic 8%
Food 65%
Other 10%
Garden 11%

Figure 4 Types of domestic waste in Bangladesh: a LIC

Recycling and disposal of waste

How is waste recycled at a local level?

Bracknell Forest Council in Berkshire works with Reading and Wokingham Councils for the disposal of waste. It has created re3 which is a waste management partnership.
Bracknell, Wokingham and Reading have two household waste recycling centres:
● Smallmead, Island Road, Reading
● Longshot Lane, Bracknell.
There are, also, 150 recycling sites around the three authorities located at convenient places such as large supermarket car parks.

How is the recycled material reused?

re3, the waste management partnership, has agreements with many different companies to recycle the waste that it collects. Below are how four of the products which are recycled by the residents are turned into usable products.

ACTIVITY

Read the information below on Bracknell.
List all the specific information about how waste is recycled and how the recycled material is used.

Cans
Cans are baled at a Biffa Waste Management facility in Southampton. They are then transferred to a reprocessing facility in Leicester. They are first split into steel and aluminium and then reused, being made into products such as cars or new cans!

Paper and cardboard
The paper and cardboard is recycled in Maidenhead. The material is sorted and baled. It is then moved to the St Regis paper mill in Kent where it is turned into new packaging material.

How do households in Bracknell recycle their waste?

Bracknell has a two-weekly collection system. One week the following are collected:
● the brown bin – garden waste
● the blue bin – plastic bottles and tins
● the green box – paper.

On the alternate week the green general waste bin is collected.

Other types of rubbish such as shoes, foil and e-waste can be taken to the household waste recycling centres.

Plastics
Plastic bottles are recycled by Baylis Recycling at their plant in Keynsham near Bristol. The bottles are sorted into different types of plastic. Products made from used plastic include garden furniture, fleece jackets and, yes, new plastic bottles.

Glass
The glass is reprocessed in Yorkshire. The glass is washed and crushed and then mixed with raw materials such as sand and limestone to make new glass containers.

How does Germany (a HIC) dispose of its domestic (municipal) waste?

Incineration
- There are 68 incinerators in Germany.
- The plant at Darmstadt incinerates 212,000 tonnes of waste a year.
- Other incinerators are mini-power plants which burn waste and provide energy to local homes and business.

Landfill
- 160 landfill sites.
- Waste has to be treated before it is allowed to be put into landfill.
- One treatment plant is owned by The Group and is sited in Luebeck in Germany. It can treat 200,000 tonnes of domestic waste annually.

14 million tonnes of municipal waste.

Recycled waste
- Germany recycles 60% of its waste.
- All products that can be recycled have the 'Grune Punkt' emblem. Buying these recyclable products costs the average family between £100 and £200 a year which has been added to their cost by the producer to pay for the recycling. Plastic, glass, paper and cardboard are all recycled. There are a number of problems with the system. The scheme is so successful that Germany cannot recycle everything that is collected. They have had to export their recyclables to other European and Asian countries. For example, plastic shampoo bottles from Oggersheim are turned into sandals in Indonesia.

ACTIVITY

Explain the ways that Germany disposes of its waste.

Exam Tip

Foundation Tier
Level 1 (1–2) A simple answer which has very little description. Could be about anywhere and not linked to any specific study.
Level 2 (3–4) A basic answer with level two being reached by there being descriptive points or a specific point or possibly a weak explanation. The top of the level requires a specific point and some linked descriptive points, or a specific point and weak explanation.
Level 3 (5–6) A clear answer with level three being reached by there being a clear explanation or a specific point. The top of the level requires a range of specific points or a number of explanations or a specific point and an explanation.

Higher Tier
Level 1 (1–2) A basic answer which has simple descriptive statements.
Level 2 (3–4) A clear answer with level two being reached by there being an explanation or a specific point. The top of the level requires a range of specific points or a number of explanations or a specific point and an explanation.
Level 3 (5–6) An explicit answer with a range of specific and explained points.

How does Germany (a HIC) dispose of nuclear waste?

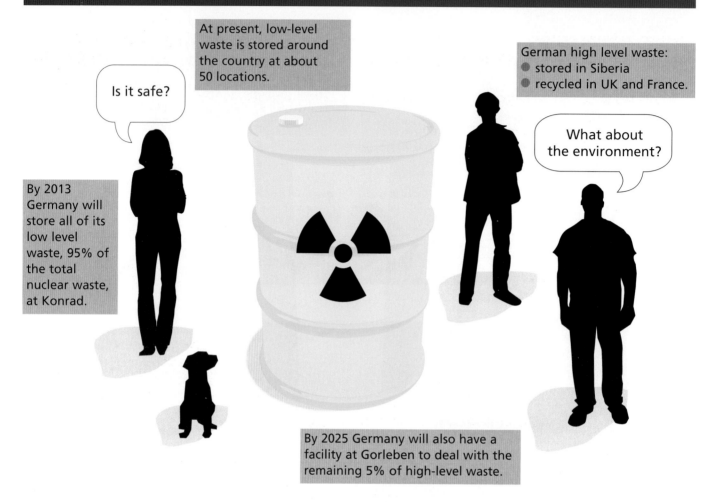

At present, low-level waste is stored around the country at about 50 locations.

Is it safe?

German high level waste:
- stored in Siberia
- recycled in UK and France.

What about the environment?

By 2013 Germany will store all of its low level waste, 95% of the total nuclear waste, at Konrad.

By 2025 Germany will also have a facility at Gorleben to deal with the remaining 5% of high-level waste.

How does Germany (a HIC) dispose of other toxic waste products?

"Don't tell me where you put it, just so long as you get rid of it."

Germany exports its toxic waste products. Between 1990 and 1995 shiploads of German toxic waste were sent to Poland, Estonia, Egypt and Albania.

During 1991 and 1992, 480 tonnes of toxic waste (pesticides) was sent to Albania. In Germany, it would have cost $5500 per tonne to dispose of the pesticides. The pesticides were sent to Albania to be used by farmers even though they were too dangerous to use in Germany.

However, within the shipment were 6000 litres of toxaphone, which is highly toxic and can kill wildlife. The Albanian government did accept the shipment but when they realised what it was they asked Germany to take it back. Eventually other world nations forced Germany to take it back. One part of the shipment was found at Bajza in Albania, where the pesticides were seeping into Lake Shkodra.

Figure 5

Sources and uses of energy

The advantages and disadvantages of renewable and non-renewable energy

Non-renewable fuels are finite resources. Once they have been used they can never be used again.

Coal + Oil + Natural gas

Non-renewable – fossil fuels
Coal is formed from fossilised plants. It can be found in seams either close to the surface or it has to be mined from deep under the ground. It has to be burnt to produce energy.

Oil is formed from fossilised animals. Lakes of oil are found under the land or sea trapped between seams of rock. Pipes are put down through the ground and the liquid is pumped to the surface. It is burnt to provide energy.

Methane gases are trapped between seams of rock under the Earth's surface. Pipes are put down through the ground and the gas is pumped to the surface. It is burnt to provide energy.

- Coal supplies should last for another 250 years.
- It is relatively easy to convert into energy by simply burning it.
- It is relatively cheap to mine.

- Oil is relatively easy to convert into energy by simply burning it.
- It is relatively cheap to mine.
- Oil supplies should last for another 50 years.

- Gas is a cleaner fuel than oil or coal giving off fewer greenhouse gases.
- Gas supplies should last for another 70 years.
- Relatively easy to convert into energy.

- Coal is bulky to transport.
- When burnt they all give off greenhouse gases, for example carbon dioxide.
- Oil can be very expensive to buy.
- Natural gas will not last forever.

Nuclear

Non-renewable
Produced from uranium which is obtained by mining. Energy is produced when the atoms are split or joined together in nuclear reactors.

- It does not give off greenhouse gases.
- Raw materials will last a long time.
- A small amount of uranium gives off a lot of energy.

- Nuclear reactors are expensive to build and run.
- Nuclear waste is radioactive and highly toxic.
- It has to be stored for 100s/1000s of years which is very expensive.

Renewable fuels are infinite resources; ones which can be reused and therefore will not run out.

Power from the ground
Ground source heat pumps take heat from the ground into the house. These supply warmth to radiators or under floor heating systems.

- It does not give off greenhouse gases.
- Cheap once built as it is an infinite resource.
- It can cut energy costs by up to 70%.

- It is expensive, costing approximately £12,000 to install.
- Enough space is needed in the garden to install the pipework.

Water
Hydroelectricity is power from water. Rivers are dammed and the flow of water is controlled. The water turns a turbine which generates electricity.

Tidal – the movement of sea water drives turbines which produce electricity.

- It does not give off greenhouse gases.
- Cheap once built as it is an infinite resource.
- Can produce large bodies of water for leisure purposes.

- It does not give off greenhouse gases.
- Cheap once built as it is an infinite resource.
- Tidal barrages can also be used as bridges.

- They alter the water flow of rivers, affecting ecology.
- Can only be built in certain areas due to dam requirements.
- 40–80 million people globally have had to move because of dam construction.

- Can be a problem for shipping if built across an estuary.
- Can be very expensive to build.
- Can negatively affect wildlife.

Wind
Turbines which rely on the force of the wind to power blades which generate electricity.

- New wind turbines are quiet and efficient. Costs £1500 for 1 kW.
- It does not give off greenhouse gases.
- Wind turbines can be on land or sea.
- Can save up to 30% of the average household's energy bill.

- There needs to be an annual local wind speed of more than 6 metres per second.
- Require regular servicing.
- They can be unsightly and visually intrusive.
- Offshore turbines may disturb migration patterns of birds.

Sun
Solar panels – fluid in panels on a roof heats up producing hot water for use.

Photovoltaic cells – these are panels or tiles which produce energy (electricity) from light, preferably sunlight.

- Can provide up to 35% of a house's hot water.
- There are no running costs.
- Fairly cheap to set up, approximately £4000 per home.
- It does not give off greenhouse gases.
- Is fitted onto buildings and therefore does not take up extra land space.

- Not efficient in countries where the sun rarely shines.
- Cannot be mass produced so is best used on a small scale.
- Photovoltaic cells cost approximately £12,000 for each home.

Energy surplus and energy deficit

- Energy surpluses are usually in LICs.
- Energy deficits are usually in HICs.

Countries have carbon footprints of differing sizes

A carbon footprint is a measure of the impact that human activities have on the environment in terms of the number of greenhouse gases they produce.

The least developed, low income countries will have the lowest carbon footprints.

The most developed, high income countries have the highest carbon footprints.

Management of energy usage and waste

How energy is being wasted – in industry

Some of the ways that British industry wastes energy:

- Office devices left running, for example computers and printers. Over the Christmas period the amount of energy wasted over the 10-day Christmas shutdown is enough to roast 4.4 million turkeys.
- Approximately £1 in every £12 spent on fuel is being wasted by the UK steel industry.
- It is estimated that £570 million is wasted on energy by industry in the UK every year.
- Poorly serviced machinery can waste a lot of energy.

How energy is being wasted – the domestic situation

The ways in which energy is wasted (and can be saved) in the domestic situation.

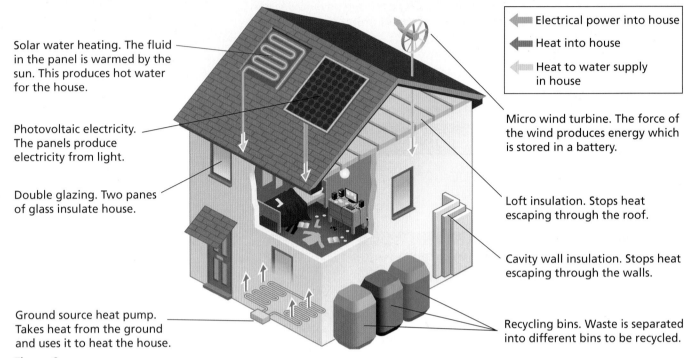

Solar water heating. The fluid in the panel is warmed by the sun. This produces hot water for the house.

Photovoltaic electricity. The panels produce electricity from light.

Double glazing. Two panes of glass insulate house.

Ground source heat pump. Takes heat from the ground and uses it to heat the house.

Figure 6

Electrical power into house

Heat into house

Heat to water supply in house

Micro wind turbine. The force of the wind produces energy which is stored in a battery.

Loft insulation. Stops heat escaping through the roof.

Cavity wall insulation. Stops heat escaping through the walls.

Recycling bins. Waste is separated into different bins to be recycled.

ACTIVITIES

1 How could energy be saved in a teenager's bedroom?
2 How do the following save energy?
   ● Fitting loft insulation.
   ● Putting a jacket on the hot-water tank.
   ● Draught proofing the windows.
   ● Fitting cavity wall insulation.

Exam Tip

If you are asked for examples on a question referring to solutions to energy wastage, ensure that you write about named places and specific information on solutions to energy wasted.

Solutions to energy wastage at a national scale

Some of the ways that the government is trying to reduce energy wastage:

● A grant of £2500 is available per household for green technologies from the Low Carbon Buildings Programme.

● There is now no need for planning permission to install wind turbines, solar panels, ground and water source heat pumps and biomass systems.

● Grants of up to £1 million for public buildings such as schools and hospitals where the government will pay up to 50% of the start-up costs. More than 200 schools have already applied to install green technologies. For example, Howe Dell Primary School in Hatfield, among other sustainable ideas, has a wind turbine, solar panels and recycles its rainwater.

Exam Tip

- **Foundation Tier** – For questions that ask for examples, your answer will be marked as follows: each point will receive a mark. If your answer does not contain a specific point about an example you will lose one mark.
- **Higher Tier** – If the command word is **outline** or **describe**, these questions will usually be marked out of four marks. Each point will receive a mark. If your answer does not include specific points about an example you will only receive two marks. If examples are asked for and you only give one you will lose one mark.

Solutions to energy wastage at a local and domestic scale

Combined Heat and Power Schemes (CHP)
Many local councils have installed CHP systems in their properties. A communal boiler produces the energy for everyone in the scheme then recovers the heat which is lost in the production of the energy and distributes it as hot water to heat houses and public buildings. There are approximately 1300 schemes in the UK. The system is up to 90% efficient, whereas some parts of the national systems are only 22% efficient. Normally gas is used as the fuel but it can be easily replaced by biofuel should the need arise.

What are local councils doing to help the domestic situation?

Wind power
Over the past 5 years there has been an increase in the number of wind turbines which can be seen around the UK. Large numbers of them feed into the National Grid. Others provide for more local electricity demands. The turbine at Green Park in Reading has been providing energy since 2005 for 1500 homes and businesses.

Reduction of council tax
British Gas is working with 16 local councils, including Reading Borough Council, to improve energy efficiency. If households implement energy efficiency measures such as loft insulation they will receive £100 off their council tax bill.

ACTIVITY

Outline the ways that energy can be saved on a local scale. Use examples in your answer.

Exam Tip

- If you are asked for examples of solutions to energy wastage at a local and domestic scale, you can use all the information about local councils on these pages. For domestic you might also like to include the information on page 46 which shows ways to make a house more energy efficient.
- For solutions to energy wasted, examples would be the initiatives that are being developed by local councils and householders.

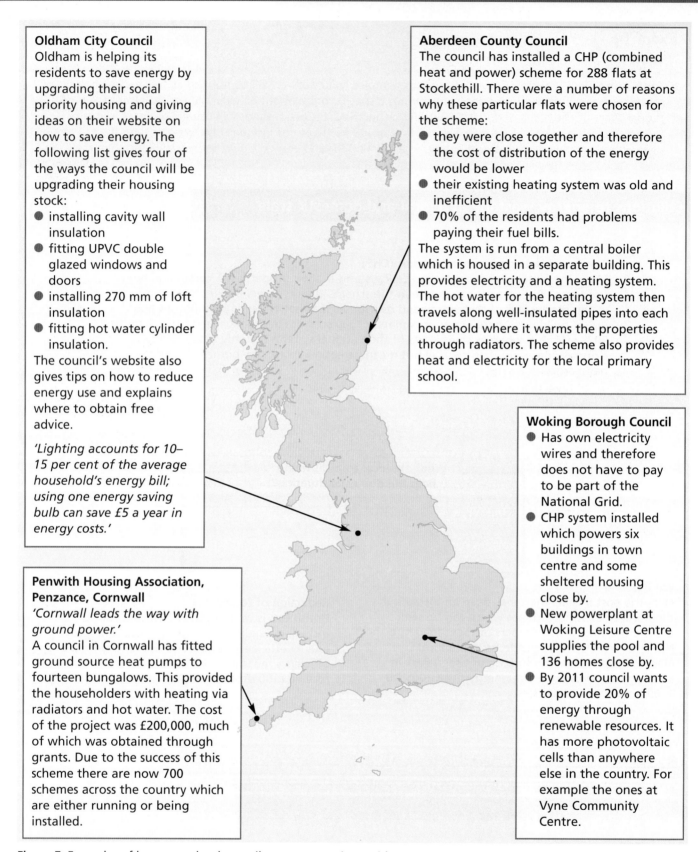

Oldham City Council
Oldham is helping its residents to save energy by upgrading their social priority housing and giving ideas on their website on how to save energy. The following list gives four of the ways the council will be upgrading their housing stock:
- installing cavity wall insulation
- fitting UPVC double glazed windows and doors
- installing 270 mm of loft insulation
- fitting hot water cylinder insulation.

The council's website also gives tips on how to reduce energy use and explains where to obtain free advice.

'Lighting accounts for 10–15 per cent of the average household's energy bill; using one energy saving bulb can save £5 a year in energy costs.'

Aberdeen County Council
The council has installed a CHP (combined heat and power) scheme for 288 flats at Stockethill. There were a number of reasons why these particular flats were chosen for the scheme:
- they were close together and therefore the cost of distribution of the energy would be lower
- their existing heating system was old and inefficient
- 70% of the residents had problems paying their fuel bills.

The system is run from a central boiler which is housed in a separate building. This provides electricity and a heating system. The hot water for the heating system then travels along well-insulated pipes into each household where it warms the properties through radiators. The scheme also provides heat and electricity for the local primary school.

Woking Borough Council
- Has own electricity wires and therefore does not have to pay to be part of the National Grid.
- CHP system installed which powers six buildings in town centre and some sheltered housing close by.
- New powerplant at Woking Leisure Centre supplies the pool and 136 homes close by.
- By 2011 council wants to provide 20% of energy through renewable resources. It has more photovoltaic cells than anywhere else in the country. For example the ones at Vyne Community Centre.

Penwith Housing Association, Penzance, Cornwall
'Cornwall leads the way with ground power.'
A council in Cornwall has fitted ground source heat pumps to fourteen bungalows. This provided the householders with heating via radiators and hot water. The cost of the project was £200,000, much of which was obtained through grants. Due to the success of this scheme there are now 700 schemes across the country which are either running or being installed.

Figure 7 Examples of how some local councils are encouraging residents to save energy

ACTIVITY

Outline the ways that energy can be saved on a local scale.
Use examples in your answer.

6   A Watery World

Water consumption and sources

There are great differences between the amount of water used in LICs, MICs and HICs. In Figure 1 each bottle represents 50 litres of water.

There are also differences in the percentage of water used in LICs and HICs domestically, agriculturally and industrially. Figure 2 shows this in more detail.

- LICS use a high proportion of their water for agriculture.

- MICs, which are often newly industrialised countries, tend to have industry as the biggest user.

- HICs use more water for domestic purposes than MICs and LICs but they still have a high proportion used in agriculture and industry.

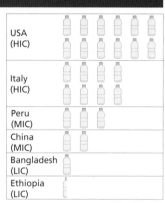

Figure 1 Water consumption per person per day

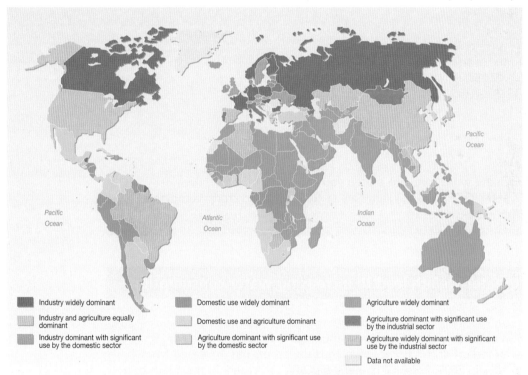

Figure 2 Water use for agriculture, industry and domestic purposes

ACTIVITIES

1. Name a country for each of the categories in Figure 2.
2. Why are so many African countries agriculture-dominant?
3. Describe the distribution of countries where industry is the widely dominant use of water.

Exam Tip

- You may be asked to describe a distribution on a map. You should start with general points.
- Your answer should then become more specific, naming countries or continents.
- If data is asked for, you will lose a mark if you don't include it.
- If data is not requested, you should still include some as you will be given credit.

Why should there be these differences?

HICs use much more water than LICs.

The reasons are summarised in the table:

	HICs	LICs
Domestic	<ul><li>Many domestic appliances such as dishwashers and washing machines</li><li>'Showering society'</li><li>All houses fitted with taps giving easy access</li></ul>	<ul><li>Clothes and dishes often washed in the river</li><li>The same water that is used for cooking or washing up is used for personal cleansing</li><li>In countries like Ghana the women have to walk 5 km to get a bucket of water for the day</li></ul>
Agricultural	<ul><li>Automated irrigation systems using 75 litres per second</li></ul>	<ul><li>Hand-worked irrigation producing 2 litres a second</li></ul>
Industrial	<ul><li>Large-scale factories</li></ul>	<ul><li>Small-scale cottage industries</li></ul>

ACTIVITY

Compare the uses of water in HICs and LICs.

Exam Tip

When the command word **compare** is used you should state the similarities between HICs and LICs. However, examiners at GCSE will also credit comments about the differences (contrasts).

How does greater wealth lead to increasing water consumption?

Domestically – Growth in sales of labour-saving machines using water. For example, the number of British homes owning dishwashers has increased from 0% in 1973 to 40% in 2009. Personal hygiene has also increased: in the 1950s one bath a week was common, nowadays many people shower daily or more if they play sport or go to a gym.

Leisure and tourism – the huge growth in the number of golf courses. There were 603 new courses built in the UK between 1990 and 2004. In southern Spain, tourists expect their hotels to have swimming pools, often filled at the expense of local people.

Where does the water we use come from on a local scale?

Aquifers

The highest level of water in an aquifer is known as the water table. The level of this varies according to whether there is a lot or a little rainfall and also if temperatures are high this can lead to water being sucked from the ground and lowering the water table.

The rainwater falling on the Chilterns and the North Downs soaks into the chalk which is a large area of porous rock. These are like giant sponges that fill up with water. They are called aquifers.

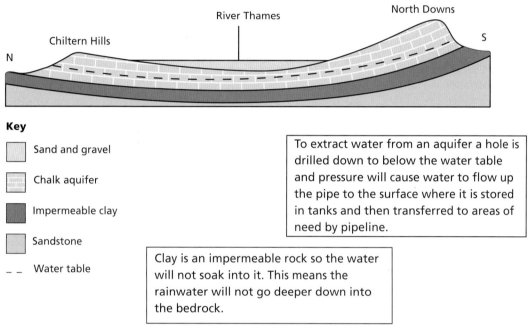

Key

	Sand and gravel
	Chalk aquifer
	Impermeable clay
	Sandstone
_ _	Water table

To extract water from an aquifer a hole is drilled down to below the water table and pressure will cause water to flow up the pipe to the surface where it is stored in tanks and then transferred to areas of need by pipeline.

Clay is an impermeable rock so the water will not soak into it. This means the rainwater will not go deeper down into the bedrock.

Figure 3 London Basin

Reservoirs

Direct supply reservoirs – store water and supply it straight to a water treatment works before it is sent to homes and businesses.

Examples:

- Hanningfield in Essex, 25 billion litres capacity, includes a wildlife Site of Special Scientific Interest (SSSI).
- King George V and William Girling reservoirs in Chingford are owned by Thames Water. A sailing club is based on the King George V reservoir and the reservoirs have been designated a SSSI because of their large bird population.

Rivers

River-regulating reservoirs – store water during rainy periods so that the river can be topped up during dry spells. This water can then be taken out further downstream at treatment plants.

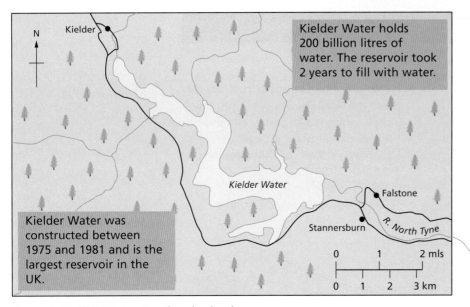

Kielder

N

Kielder Water holds 200 billion litres of water. The reservoir took 2 years to fill with water.

Kielder Water

Falstone

Stannersburn

R. North Tyne

Kielder Water was constructed between 1975 and 1981 and is the largest reservoir in the UK.

0   1   2 mls

0   1   2   3 km

Figure 4 Kielder Water, Northumberland

R. North Tyne

Water is extracted at the treatment works at Horsley and Mosswood for use in Newcastle.

R. Wear

Water is extracted at the treatment works at Lumley for use in Sunderland.

R. Tees

Water is extracted at the treatment works at Broken Scar for use in Middlesbrough.

ACTIVITIES

1 What are the problems that might be caused when a reservoir is built?

2 Suggest why reservoirs are built where they are?

Why do water supplies vary?

- Some places have a surplus and some a deficit (scarcity).
- Distribution of rainfall is uneven around the world.
- Some areas have high evapotranspiration rates so rainwater is quickly taken back into the atmosphere.
- Major desert areas have a physical water deficit (scarcity) because they have low rainfall and high evaporation rates.
- Many African and South American countries suffer an economic scarcity because they cannot afford to access available water.

Exam Tip

You will need to be able to describe patterns and compare and contrast what the maps show. Be able to give reasons for the differences between countries with water surplus and water deficit.

Water supply problems

What are the problems associated with water supply in HICs?

The availability of water is determined by the quality, spatial and seasonal variability and the amount of water lost through broken pipes.

Problems	HICs
Quality	<ul><li>Factories give off gases that mix with water, and ultimately this causes problems with water pollution. Run-off from agricultural operations can potentially release fertiliser into water sources, which contain harmful chemicals.</li><li>Hard water contains minerals such as calcium and magnesium. These minerals impair its quality, as calcium may cause soap scum to form in bathrooms, as well as leaving behind deposits known as limescale.</li><li>Hard water may also give a lower quality taste due to the fact that there are low levels of chlorine present.</li></ul>
Spatial variability	<ul><li>The population and the rainfall of the UK are unevenly distributed. One-third of the UK's population lives in south-east England but this is also the driest part of the UK with average annual rainfall of less than 800 mm.</li><li>The least populated areas of the UK are in the mountain areas of Scotland, Wales and north-west England, but it is here that the most rain falls, over 2000 mm.</li></ul>
Seasonal variability	<ul><li>There is a problem with the seasonal supply of water in many of the Mediterranean holiday areas (see Figure 5).</li><li>Murcia, in southern Spain, has undergone a resort-building boom which caused problems in 2008. Farmers were fighting developers over water rights because their crops were short of water. They were buying and selling water like gold on a rapidly growing black market, mostly from illegal wells.</li></ul>
Leakage	<ul><li>In London, more than half of the water mains are more than 100 years old, and around a third are over 150.</li><li>30% of the water supply is lost through leaks and cracks. In 2006 more than 3.5 billion litres of water were lost daily through broken and leaking pipes in England and Wales.</li><li>The water that leaks daily through broken pipes is a loss to the economy of between £1,512,000 and £3,600,000 because this is how much it will cost to retreat the water to make it drinkable.</li></ul>

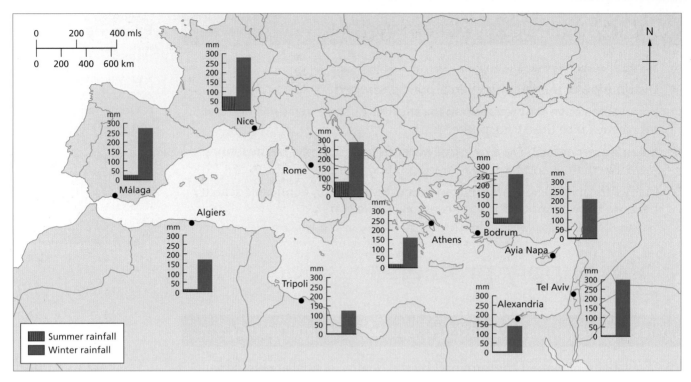

Figure 5 Seasonal water supply in the Mediterranean

ACTIVITY

What does Figure 5 show about seasonal water imbalance along the Mediterranean coastline?

What are the problems associated with water supply in LICs?

Problems	LICs
Clean piped water	● The greatest problem in LICs is the high proportion of the population that does not have access to clean piped water. ● One billion people in LICs do not have access to safe water; this is roughly one-sixth of the world's population.
Water-related diseases	● Intestinal worms infect about 10% of the population of LICs. Parasites that infect the intestine can lead to malnutrition, anaemia and stunted growth. ● 1.8 million children die every year as a result of diseases caused by unclean water and poor sanitation. This amounts to around 5000 deaths a day. ● At any given time, almost half the population of LICs is suffering from one or more of the main diseases associated with inadequate provision of water and sanitation. ● Dirty contaminated water is responsible for a range of health problems including dysentery, malaria, bilharzia and trachoma.
Pollution	● Many of the indigenous tribes in the Amazon region have suffered from water contamination due to mining operations and oil exploitation. ● Unlined waste pits provide a major source of pollution in the Oriente region of Ecuador. Since there are no other options for obtaining water, local people now depend on these contaminated sources for drinking water. ● Thousands of people are slowly poisoning themselves as they drink the water and wash and bathe in local streams. This has led to increased risks of cancer, miscarriage, dermatitis, fungal infection, headaches and nausea. Childhood leukaemia rates are four times higher in this area than in other parts of Ecuador; children as young as a few months have died of leukaemia.

Management of water usage and resources

How is water usage being managed in HICs

Domestic

A wide range of examples of water management which can be used in the home:

- metering
- short flush toilets
- hosepipe bans
- showering, instead of bathing
- economy settings on dishwashers and washing machines
- greywater used on the garden
- rain collection for watering the garden.

Industrial

Many companies are using water-saving techniques to conserve water. Walkers Crisps has reduced its use of water by 50%. This has saved 700 million litres of water a year:

- They installed 30 water meters at their production plants.
- They are recycling water from the starch recovery programme for use in another part of the production process.
- They also re-educated their staff about the use of water in the sanitation facilities. Water usage is now monitored per shift. 'Leak busters' and 'water champions' are assigned to each shift.

Cadbury Trebor Bassett is committed to saving water. They have reduced water usage at the site by about 15% per year, saving 17 million litres per year:

- Reusing waste water. The company has installed an on-site waste water treatment plant, at a cost of £2 million, to clean water that has been through the production process. This water can then be reused in a variety of different ways, for example in the cooling towers.

Agricultural

There are several ways that water can be used more efficiently in farming:

- Drip irrigation is the most efficient as it delivers water straight to the plant roots with minimal losses. It is however very expensive.
- Rainfall sensors can be used so that crops are only watered when they need it.
- Creating furrows in the fields to retain water and to prevent run-off.

How is water usage being managed in LICs?

Appropriate technology schemes for water supply are being developed in LICs:

- hand-dug wells
- rainwater harvesting
- gravity-fed schemes
- tubewells and boreholes
- recycling.

ACTIVITY

Outline the main features of each of the appropriate technology water schemes in the list.

How can water transfers cause conflicts?

A case study of the Tigris–Euphrates river system

The Southeastern Anatolia Project (GAP) will create 21 dams in Turkey. The Ataturk Dam is the key structure for the development of the Lower Euphrates River region. This will restrict flow to Syria and Iraq.

The main problem is that both the Tigris and the Euphrates have their source in Turkey and then flow through Syria and Iraq

Turkey has created several dams which are restricting the flow of water into Syria and Iraq.

Since only some of the GAP irrigation project has been finished, disputes between Turkey and Iraq are likely to increase as less water will flow into Iraq.

In Syria the Tabaqah Dam forms a reservoir, Lake Assad, that is used for irrigating cotton. Syria has dammed its two tributaries and is in the process of constructing another dam. The scarcity of water in the Middle East leaves Iraq in constant fear that Syria and Turkey will use up most of the water before it reaches Iraq.

Turkey argues that GAP is beneficial to Syria and Iraq, as the flow of the rivers is now more constant. However this has not happened. After GAP the waters of the Euphrates will decrease from 30 billion cubic metres a year (BCM/a) at the Syrian border to 16 BCM/a, and at the Iraqi border from 16 BCM/a to 5 BCM/a.

Black Sea

TURKEY

Ataturk Dam

SYRIA

Mediterranean Sea

Tabaqah Dam

Tigris R.

Euphrates R.

IRAN

IRAQ

Persian Gulf

Key
■ Dams

- Conflict in this area has been ongoing since the 1940s.
- In 1974 Iraq put troops on the Syrian border and threatened to destroy Syria's Al-Thawra Dam on the Euphrates.
- Talks are continuing but there was great tension at the conference on international law over shared water resources in the Arab region, held at Sharm-el-Sheik in May 2000.

Developments in 2009
In March 2009 Turkey promised to double the amount of water to flow downstream to Iraq. This did not happen. Iraq relies on the river water for 90% of its irrigation needs. The Iraqi government has not allowed rice farmers in the southern part of the country to plant their crops. In the city of Najaf farmers demonstrated and demanded that the government force Turkey to release more water. The amount of water in the Euphrates flowing out of Turkey is a quarter of what it was in 2000. Conflicts between Iraq and Turkey are certain to increase in the future.

The Three Gorges water management scheme

ACTIVITY

Explain the effects of the Three Gorges Water management scheme.

Reasons for the scheme

→ Produce electricity for rapidly growing industrial areas. The total electric generating capacity of the dam will reach 22,500 megawatts.

Control flooding along the Yangtze floodplain which will stop huge areas of farmland from being destroyed.

Improve shipping. The new navigable waterways along the Yangtze will provide mass transit of raw materials to the area allowing massive economic growth. They have allowed container shipping to reach all the way up the Yangtze River from Shanghai to Chongqing, the biggest city of south-west China. The river transport will be improved from 10 million to 50 million tonnes per year and the costs reduced by 35%. Navigation on the Yangtze River will become much easier in the drier season when water levels used to be low.

	Effects on people	Effects on environment
Positive effects	• New industry will bring jobs for the local people. • Tourism has brought jobs to the locals. Ex-farmers are now being used in the tourist industry, for example the Tujia, a local ethnic minority, now cater for tourists by dragging small boats by rope along the Shennong stream, to allow the tourists access to beautiful scenery. • More than 800,000 tourists visited the Three Gorges Dam area in 2007, with tourism revenue of £10 million. • It will protect the lives and property of 15 million people from flooding.	• It will have a flood control capacity of 22.15 billion cubic metres, which will be sufficient to control the greatest flood experienced in the past 100 years. • It will protect 1,500,000 hectares of farmland.
Negative effects	• 1.4 million people have had to move because their villages and towns have been lost beneath the rising waters. • Gaoyang was the last town to be evacuated in July 2008. • In July 2007 a hillside collapsed, dragging 13 farmers to their deaths and drowning 11 fishermen. • A big mudslide hit a village in the Gaoyang area in April 2008, sweeping into the local school's playground and part of the village. In July 2008, a landslide in Badong County in Hubei Province, beside the reservoir, killed more than 30 people after burying a bus.	• The Yangtze River dolphin has become extinct. • Large wetland area that attracted the Siberian Crane has been destroyed. • Numbers of the Yangtze sturgeon have gone down. • The water quality of the Yangtze's tributaries is deteriorating rapidly, as the dammed river is less able to disperse pollutants effectively. • Landslides are commonplace, the reservoir has already collapsed in 91 places and a total of 36 km have caved in.

Exam Tip

Foundation Tier
Level 1 (1–2) A simple answer which has very little description. Could be about anywhere and not linked to any specific study.
Level 2 (3–4) A basic answer with level two being reached by there being descriptive points or a specific point or possibly a weak explanation. The top of the level requires a specific point and some linked descriptive points, or a specific point and weak explanation.
Level 3 (5–6) A clear answer with level three being reached by there being a clear explanation or a specific point. The top of the level requires a range of specific points or a number of explanations or a specific point and an explanation.

Higher Tier
Level 1 (1–2) A basic answer which has simple descriptive statements.
Level 2 (3–4) A clear answer with level two being reached by there being an explanation or a specific point. The top of the level requires a range of specific points or a number of explanations or a specific point and an explanation.
Level 3 (5–6) An explicit answer with a range of specific and explained points.

Exam support

Command words

Command words are words that are used in exam questions. They ask you to do something specific. Examiners do not write questions to catch you out; they want you to be able to answer them.

If you understand what is meant by the command words then you will be able to answer the questions accurately and not waste time writing things that are irrelevant.

- **Compare**
  Say in what way two or more things are alike, or different from each other. You should use comparative words such as 'It has a similar height to …' 'larger than', 'faster flowing than' or 'more vegetation than'.

- **Contrast**
  Say in what way two or more things are different from each other. This is very like the command word compare, but the difference is that you should not state any similarities.

- **Define**
  You may be asked to define a term. The examiner will be expecting you to state the meaning of that term in a geographical framework.

- **Describe**
  This is a very common command word and requires you to give the main characteristics of something. Questions will often ask you to describe a photograph, a pattern on a graph or a map. You should write an accurate account of what you see. You are trying to represent in words the picture you see to the examiner.

- **Name, give, identify or state**
  These words require you to answer briefly and are usually only worth one mark. For example, 'Give the grid reference for …' or 'Name one type of sea defence'.

- **Use data in your answer**
  This is often used with the command word describe. In this case, you must use data (information) in your answer.
  For example, if you were asked to describe the population distribution on a map using data in your answer, it would not be good enough to say there are lots of people in one area and not many in another. You would use the figures provided on the map to make specific factual comments on each area. It may help your answer even if not specifically asked for.

- **Discuss**
  If you are asked to discuss something you will be expected to bring forward the important points of the argument.

- **Estimate**
  In some cases you may be asked to estimate a distance, which means to give an approximate value.

- **Explain**
  This is another very common command word. It is asking you to give reasons as to why something occurs. It is testing your ability to understand how something happens.
  For example, the farmer keeps sheep on the hillside because of the infertile soil and cooler climate.

- **Justify**
  You may be required to justify your answer to a previous question, possibly using a map or photograph. In this instance, you must state the case for your answer – in other words, give reasons for your answer.

- **Outline**
  If you are asked to outline something, you will be expected to summarise the main points. You may at times use explanation in this answer which will be credited, but the examiner is looking to see how well you have summarised the main characteristics of the particular feature.

- **Suggest/give reasons for**
  This is similar to explain but sometimes there are varying reasons why something happens and there is not necessarily a right or wrong answer. The examiner will expect you to give more than one reason.

For example, a farmer will grow a crop for a number of reasons and these could be physical or human.

● **Annotate**
This means to give a descriptive comment and an explanation. This is often used on landform formation questions such as 'Use only an annotated diagram or diagrams'.

● **Label**
This is simple descriptive comment which identifies something.

● **Rank**
This means to put the answers into the correct order; you may also be required to justify your order.

Other command words such as draw and complete will also be used, such as 'Complete the field sketch' or 'Draw a diagram'.

Sample exam questions

There follows a number of answers to examination questions. They have been marked according to the mark schemes that are provided in this revision guide. These are the mark schemes that will be used to mark your answer when you do your examination.

The first example is for a case study question on a water transfer scheme which is part of A Watery World topic (see page 56 in Chapter 6).

Foundation Tier
Disputes can occur over water transfers. For one water transfer scheme outline the disputes.
(6 marks)

Higher Tier
Disputes can occur over water transfers. For one water transfer scheme explain the disputes.
(6 marks)

Student answer

Some countries use dams to help conserve water but this often results in disputes over money and the water. In Turkey a dam was made to conserve some of the water in a nearby river. This caused disputes with Iraq and Syria. They wanted water for their crops. The dams in Turkey stopped the water flowing downstream.

Exam Tip

Foundation Tier – Level 2 (3 marks).
This would achieve three marks on Foundation Tier. No specific case study facts are mentioned.

Higher Tier – This would achieve level 1 (2 marks).
No specific case study facts are mentioned
No explanation, only several simple descriptive statements.

The Euphrates river has caused many conflicts between Turkey, Iraq and Syria because Iraq relies on 90% of its irrigation water from this river. The farmers in Iraq are struggling to grow their crops. It is becoming harder for Iraq to receive enough water due to Turkey building 21 dams with GAP and because of this only a quarter of the water leaves their country. Syria has also built dams (Tabaqah) which are restricting flow to Iraq. The GAP project has reduced the water flowing to Iraq from 16 billion cubic metres to 5 billion cubic metres.

Exam Tip

Foundation Tier – Level 3 (6 marks).

Higher Tier – This would achieve level 3 (5 marks).
There is a range of specific facts. However, the explanation although present is weak. Therefore the answer does not reach full marks.

The Southern Anatolian project is a prime example of how disputes can happen over water transfer. The Tigris–Euphrates is a major source of water for Turkey, Syria and Iraq. As the source of the water is in Turkey they are in control. They built dams restricting the water flow to Syria and even more to Iraq. So whilst water is so scarce in Iraq there are no signs of a water shortage in Turkey. Iraq has become unhappy with the restrictions as it makes irrigation water less available and problems arise with growing crops.

Exam Tip

Foundation Tier – Level 2 (3 marks). Three marks because although it is a good answer at this level there is no specific case study detail.

Higher Tier – This would achieve level 2 (3 marks). There are two explanations which means that the answer is in level two but they are weak explanations and so not good enough for the top of this level.

This example is for a case study question on river management which is part of the River Landscapes topic (see page 21 in Chapter 2).

In 1998 the River Nene flooded. To manage the river, an embankment was built at Weeden at a cost of £2 million so water can be stored here, preventing flooding. Also 4 m floodwalls have been built at Footmeadow to protect housing and industry in the area. This increases the capacity of the channel, preventing flooding. The channel was widened by 12 m near the railway station. Also, here debris was cleared so the river velocity increases so there is less friction, less material deposited, and rainwater is taken away quicker. Gabion boxes were also added. This is all hard engineering. Soft engineering included a flood retention reservoir at Billing where cattle can graze in spring. Also, at Upton, earth embankments covered in grass were built which are very natural looking. They are set 10 m from the river increasing the channel capacity at times of flood.

Hint! Specific case study facts are in red. Explanations are in purple.

Exam Tip

Higher Tier – This would achieve level 3 (6 marks). An explicit answer with a range of specific case study facts and explained points.

This example is for a case study question on coastal management which is part of the Coastal Landscapes topic (see page 11 in Chapter 1).

The cliffs are being managed in different ways. In November 1998, £167,000 was paid by the local council for 300 tonnes of Leicester granite to be placed on the beach. It was put there to protect the cliff close to the Tower. It has only managed to slow down erosion, not to stop it. Drainage channels have been installed underground on the graded cliff to enable water to flow through the rocks and into the sea so that the slope does not get waterlogged and slump. The slope has also been planted with nettles and brambles to stop people scrambling on the cliff. The sea wall was built in 1977 to protect the cliff, and groynes were also built in 1977 to stop longshore drift and sand moving from south to north along the beach.

Exam Tip

Higher Tier – This would achieve level 3 (6 marks). An explicit answer with a range of specific case study facts and explained points.

This example is for a landform formation question which is part of the River Landscapes topic (see page 14 in Chapter 2).

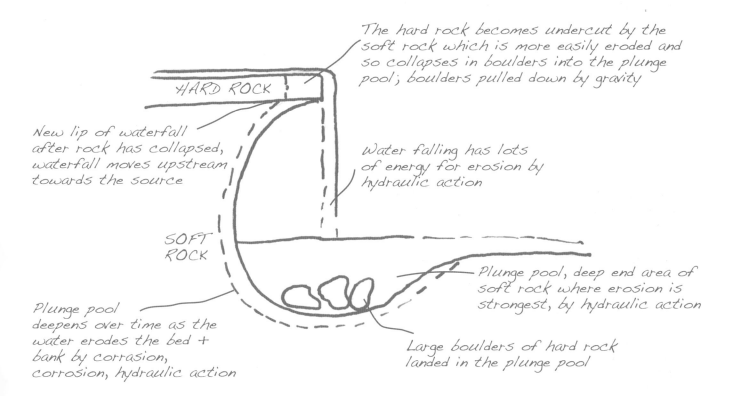

The hard rock becomes undercut by the soft rock which is more easily eroded and so collapses in boulders into the plunge pool; boulders pulled down by gravity

New lip of waterfall after rock has collapsed, waterfall moves upstream towards the source

HARD ROCK

Water falling has lots of energy for erosion by hydraulic action

SOFT ROCK

Plunge pool, deep end area of soft rock where erosion is strongest, by hydraulic action

Plunge pool deepens over time as the water erodes the bed + bank by corrasion, corrosion, hydraulic action

Large boulders of hard rock landed in the plunge pool

Exam Tip

Higher Tier – 4 marks.
The answer has a full sequence, with several descriptive points and two explanations although one would be enough. There is a named process (hydraulic action), explanation is not required.

This example is for a landform formation question which is part of the
Coastal Landscapes topic (see page 4 in Chapter 1).

The arch was formed by erosion of the rock by the sea. It will have started with
a crack. When the sea crashed against the rock the crack would fill with air at a
high pressure and when the waves retreated the pressure would be released,
taking fragments of rock with it. Eventually the crack would become so large due
to the hydraulic action (the air pressure in the cracks) that a cave would be
formed. If on a headland, caves would form either side and eventually, due to
erosion would meet in the middle forming an arch like the one shown. The headland
would get more of the waves' energy as it sticks out into the sea with nothing
protecting it which is why the arch probably formed here.

In the future, erosion will continue to occur with perhaps corrasion where debris
will be thrown at the bottom of the rock by the sea till the top of the arch gets
pulled down by gravity. This will cause a stack to be formed. Eventually this
may also turn into a slump as more erosion occurs.

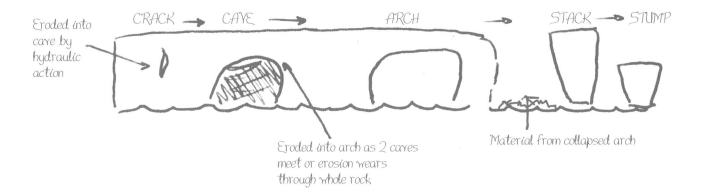

Eroded into cave by hydraulic action

CRACK → CAVE → ARCH → STACK → STUMP

Eroded into arch as 2 caves meet or erosion wears through whole rock

Material from collapsed arch

Exam Tip

Higher Tier – 4 marks.
This has process and sequence explained but would
still receive four marks as that is the maximum for
the question.